D1605906

Spiritual Life Studies

by

Harold Ewing Burchett

Published by the Author

Printed in the United States of America

Table of Contents

Preface to the Second Edition v

Introduction 1

Part 1   Getting Acquainted with SLS

   I. God Says Do It, So Let's Obey 9

   II. The SLS Procedure — What Will Be Happening to You .. 11

  III. Final Instructions Before Launching 14

Part 2   SLS Lessons

     I. John 1 and 2 19

    II. John 3 and 4 24

   III. John 5 29

   IV. John 6 and 7 36

    V. John 8 and 9 41

   VI. John 10 and 11 48

  VII. John 12 and 13 55

 VIII. John 14 and 15 62

   IX. John 16 and 17 69

    X. John 18 and 19 74

   XI. John 20, Colossians 3:1-5 79

  XII. Romans 6, 7, 8 87

 XIII. Romans 8, John 21 94

Part 3   The Leader's Preparation

   I. Objectives: Know What You Are Trying to Accomplish 103

  II. Grasping the Mechanics of this Technique 110

      Arranging with a Partner 110

      Preparing to Serve 111

      Conducting the Study 114

      The Place of Prayer in Each Session 118

      The Final Session — What Next? 118

      Other Questions in Your Mind 119

  III. Additional Teachings 121

      Additional Areas of Christian Living to Check 121

      Additional Insights into the Scripture Lessons 122

  IV. Special Helps for Saying it Simply 131

Preface to the Second Edition

Over many years, God has blessed the use of Spiritual Life Studies, in its first edition. Recent translations into Japanese and Spanish have expanded the ministry. Work on some other languages is in various stages of planning.

This new edition uses the New International Version of the Bible. In addition to numerous minor changes (largely for added clarity), three significant additions appear in the second edition. In Lesson XII at Romans 6:2 and following verses, several paragraphs have been inserted. My purpose is to show even more clearly that the Apostle is speaking in that section about the settlement of sin as legal guilt and *not* about our "deadness" to the pull of sin.

"The Place of Prayer in Each Session" is now included in Part 3, "The Leader's Preparation," as one of the vital "Mechanics of this Technique."

The other significant addition is also in Part 3 and involves several new sentences included in the brief definition of "Sin," under "Special Helps for Saying It Simply."

May our Lord Jesus Christ bless all that honors Him.

Harold E. Burchett

Introduction

Rather than dreaming of an elusive spiritual awakening that never seems to come, here is the pick and shovel of revival — a practical way of getting out in the trenches and seeing something happen.

Years ago in the Navy I watched the cook mount a ladder to the huge soup vats and stir them with a paddle of considerable size. Now, I picture many of today's pastors and Christian workers desperately trying to stir an oversize kettle with their own small spoons. New techniques of dipping, plunging, splashing away with the spoon are not needed. What is needed is a larger paddle! This deeper stirring will take place when the pastor broadens the base of ministry by multiplying himself. Many other Christians can be trained individually to become personal edifiers in the church.

When men and women are dealt with individually, how different are the results from what is usually obtained in a class or through the congregational approach. This more personal, intensive method is often little short of wonderful in its effect. The workman will, however, have to keep his faith alive and put in real sustained labor.

Two distinctives mark the spiritual life studies that I will be sharing with you. First, the serious manner in which all the teachings are taken directly from the open Bible and applied to the life. Secondly, because of the personal exchange and questions between the leader and his partner, all applications are immediately adjusted and fitted to the life of the partner. This approach will not then be viewed as a set course of content to which the recipient must be exposed but a manner of using Biblical truth in preparing a life to become permanently fruitful.

The spiritual life studies are a composite of doctrine and duty woven together. The movement is from truth to response. Selected texts, generally from the single book of John, become successive centers of teaching around which the couple focuses discussion and determines appropriate life response. As truths are repeated and dealt with more deeply week by week, definite evidence of growth is sought in the attitudes and actions. The results must show in life's various arenas.

Given in conversational style, the blending of instruction and admonition, doctrine and duty, as they issue from selected texts, should deeply affect all who share in the lessons. Every sincere participant should become more open spiritually, more sensitive to the needs of others, and more prepared for spiritual fellowship and service.

Admittedly, it is difficult to encourage a faltering brother or sister in Christ by making repeated appointments and planning what to say and do each time. Far better to have a plan and simply enlist a partner to share the series of fellowship meetings with you.

I believe every Christian should have the studies — new believers, those moving into the area from another church fellowship, the indifferent, weak or fallen. Perhaps it is even more important that the regular members of the church — especially officers and leaders — should have this help. The most used are often the least ministered to. All too many in the church are virtually without personal shepherding for their heart needs. Surely a limited staff cannot care for all. Here is a way to discover and develop spiritual equipment in many additional lives.

The Church fellowship might be viewed as concentric circles. Place the people of little contact with the Church out on the periphery and continue the target with circles of increased interest and involvement, picturing the leaders on the bull's eye surrounded immediately by the regulars of the church. Now, let the pastor and those in responsibility stand before this picture and ask themselves where their time and interest are invested. Unto whom are they ministering? If the heart of the leadership is kept right, help in healing will radiate outward, affecting and evangelizing those outside the fold. However, the periphery should not get an undue amount of shepherding energy from those at the very center.

The whole idea of one believer meeting with another for purposes of spiritual upbuilding is taught in the New Testament. Paul commended the Roman believers because they were "competent to instruct one another" (Romans 15:14). He himself followed the same approach as he testifies in 1 Thessalonians 2:11. Further Biblical warrant for individuals upbuilding one another is given in Romans 14:19; Colossians 1:28, 3:16; 1 Thessalonians 4:18, 5:11; Titus 2; Hebrews 3:13, 10:24.

The ultimate goal of the Spiritual Life Studies is not only to edify individuals through this approach but also to discover and equip faithful ones who can become regular leaders of SLS. Even when dealing with such individuals, it is of utmost importance to avoid giving them the impression, "I am telling you these things so you can pass them on to others in need." No, at all times I must feel that each one with whom I work has needs and should himself be helped. Later, those who are willing can be trained as leaders.

Training those who will lead SLS will require special effort and some supervision. Here is a place where pastors or others who can take responsibility over fellow workers can multiply themselves and keep the ministry of edification going forward. Comparatively few Christians will persevere through this Manual on their own unless led and helped by others who are "self starters." If you have this inner drive from the Holy Spirit to function yourself and also the ability to stir others to their service, then, may God help you consider stimulating Spiritual Life Studies in your circle.

One attempting to read nonstop through this Manual will miss the purpose of it all. It is imperative that the sessions presented in the main section (Part 2) be approached in accordance with the instruction given in the preparatory Part 1.

If the ax is dull and its edge unsharpened, more strength is needed but skill will bring success. (Eccl. 10:10).

The mocker seeks wisdom and finds none, but knowledge comes easily to the discerning. (Prov. 14:6).

After many years (nearly half a century) of questioning individuals, close up and quite personally, I have found a painful ignorance of basic doctrine and inability (if not unwillingness) to practice the precepts of Scripture. This means that to some degree there is an element of charade in our modern life. A dangerous game, indeed! These studies, then, are dedicated to remedying that, one person at a time. Soon there will be many who can help. But still the process will go on, one-to-one. This seemingly long way is the short way to a lasting revival in the church and is, after all, the Biblical way.

At first these lessons spread about with very little set down in any finished form. What has proven effective in experience is now committed to writing in this book. SLS has been used on campus, military base, prison, mission field, but it is especially planned for the local church.

Over the years, the results of SLS in many individual cases have been truly remarkable and, in most cases, excellent.

4

The accumulative effect in churches where employed broadly has been very heartening indeed and characterized by depth and permanency.

Part 1

Getting Acquainted With SLS

I

God Says Do It, So Let's Obey

An often forgotten truth lives somewhat hidden behind indefinite translations at this address, 1 Thess. 2:11. The key phrase here is rendered by Phillips: "We dealt with each one of you personally." And, by the New English Bible: "We dealt with you one by one."

The very nature of church life as ordered in Scripture demands continual, personal edification. Such Bible terms as counsel, admonish, exhort, rebuke, warn, instruct, encourage, comfort and the like make it our obligation to build up our friends.

The plan of the Spiritual Life Studies is for two individuals to meet together for thirteen weekly sessions of one hour length for mutual and guided edification. This will mean a treatment of the entire Christian life using Bible doctrine for that purpose. In the role as your leader, I will be trying to discover what you know and what you do about what you know. Do you have inner struggles with your disposition, attitudes, inner purity, or in making right choices? Are you faithful at work or school? How deeply have Christian teachings affected your courtship or marriage and family life? What views do you have of God himself? And, what is the state of health of your relationship with him? As we share these studies, often punctuated with questions and admonitions, you should experience an important upturn in your life with God. Faithfully persevere then.

Let me put the SLS in perspective. As you probably know, both individual Christians and church congregations in time tend to lose vitality and bog down. Even with the newer vibrant believers and congregations, gravitation seems downward after a number of years. What is the answer?

A reliable ongoing plan of upbuilding individuals will meet the need. Public ministry is important, but personal, individual ministry is also absolutely essential.

Perhaps it could be said there are four kinds of the edification that ought to be taking place continually in the lives of believers. First, there is public instruction and encouragement in planned messages. Then, there is public edification of the spontaneous sort, where members in an assembly rise in testimony or exhortation to one another. Thirdly, individuals need to speak helpfully to one another before and after services and in daily contacts as occasion allows.

Finally, there is that fourth kind of edification, with which we are concerned — a plan of prepared fellowship between two individuals. This scheme ought to canvas every area of doctrine and the practical life responses appropriate to these truths. When doctrine and duty are properly integrated and shared helpfully from one individual to another, it ought to be a life-changing experience.

No attempt will be made to present a diet of systematic theology. That has its place. But personal, spiritual growth is nurtured best by more gradual instruction in the various truths, cycling back over the same ground, and each time a bit more deeply. This advantage can be offered when there is a schedule of weekly studies between individuals. This allows the leader to make a dynamic tailoring of the truths to the needs of his partner.

II
The SLS Procedure -
What Will Be Happening to You

Do you enjoy being asked questions? That is what I shall do continually throughout this guide. Please allow it!

When you read Scripture do you see with clarity what God is trying to get across to you personally? Is your response definite and wholehearted? Can you put those lessons into clear, winning words to others?

I shall attempt to assist you in looking over a Scripture text and both naming and understanding the particular truth taught or implied. No sloshing will be allowed. Duty must not be blurred with doctrine but founded upon it. Hopefully, you will come to a new comprehension, appropriation and expression of God's great truths.

Now, let me make clear how we shall proceed together. Throughout this Manual you will be my partner. If this is your first time in the studies, please understand that it is not the most ideal procedure to miss the person to person experience for yourself. (Perhaps after you finish, God will lead you to guide another person through the sessions rather than simply hand him the Manual!) Therefore, to gain full advantage you ought to picture the two of us seated together each time you take up the studies. Make certain you are prepared with Bible, paper and pen — as you will be instructed in the next chapter.

If by any chance you already have had a Christian friend guide you through these sessions, then I will be to you a trainer in a refresher course. You will be looking over my shoulder as I deal with another. Please keep this in mind as you proceed.

You will be asked to commit yourself in written reply to key questions. Two benefits will come to you from this. First, you will be forced to express what you think and believe and to see how it contrasts with teachings that follow. Second, as you review your notes later on, you will recognize definite evidences of growth and alterations, to God's glory.

Before beginning Part 2, I again urge you to seek one who has completed the studies to lead you. Where possible, the personal encounter is much to be preferred. Otherwise, go forward prayerfully, cooperating with all the instructions, and God will bless you. I shall try to be as clear and helpful as possible.

Readily enough it will be seen that we are not launching a series of weekly meetings of fluffy fellowship. Instead, I shall without apology be direct and open with you, hoping to change your life. Also, as leader, I would expect to be blessed myself in the effort.

It will be apparent that we're using Scriptures in the book of John. I must warn you, however, that this will not in any way be a book study. Rather, you ought to think of each succeeding text as a campfire of truth around which we shall sit for brief discussion and heart examination. Then we shall rise and move quickly to another. Sometimes we will not pause to look at many of the grand teachings along the way, between our stops. Keep remembering that our purpose is not to teach the book of John. Hopefully, you will have other opportunities to share systematically its vast riches. We shall also avoid the temptation to devotionalize on various themes, praying instead that the Spirit will make the selected truths keen-edged, practical and life changing.

At all costs, I will attempt to lead you away from merely collecting a body of teachings to pass along to another. I wish very much to have you be a hearty recipient of each teaching. You're not now learning how to use a tool. First, you must submit yourself to the edge of that tool, which is the Word of the Living God. Little will be accomplished if you are unwilling to accept this position.

III
Final Instructions Before Launching

Two temptations will confront you immediately as you begin. You will want to read ahead in the book. However, it will not make very good reading for one who has not completed the studies. The exercise of facing the questions and meeting God at each new stage is the key to SLS. Be sure to limit your reading to the designated material.

Perhaps for now you will be satisfied to know that you are standing on the launching pad with very few paragraphs separating between you and the opening session. The thirteen lessons comprising Part 2 of this Manual must be covered, one per week. The concluding Part 3 must for now remain closed to you, unless you are directed in one of the sessions to the Special Helps section. Part 3 will become familiar ground once you have completed the main sessions and are attempting to lead others where you have walked.

A second temptation for some will be to explore the many Scripture sections skipped over in our procedure — particularly in the Gospel of John. Remember that our aim is to select truths which bear on that aspect of Christian life under discussion. We are not attempting to master the book of John as such.

As you begin Lesson 1, try to reserve one quiet hour for Bible search, facing my questions with frank, written answers and enjoying moments of prayer. After completing each lesson, take a week for the simple assignments and for pondering and growing in the truths I have shared. Now, here are the important, final instructions for launching:

Open your Bible to the Gospel of John. Where not otherwise indicated, all references will be from John in the New International Version.

Have in hand a pen and a good notebook — preferably loose leaf of the half-sheet size. In each chapter several questions will be printed in **bold type**. As these are asked, quickly jot down your answer to each one. Sometimes I will give the answer right in the main text as you continue reading. Or, you might see it immediately in the Scripture. Other questions will be answered in a special answer section.

This answer section will appear at the bottom of the page and will contain needed teaching for key questions. Shield this section from your view until you have committed your response in writing. Then, check my instruction in the lower section. Where you fail to get a right answer, do not destroy what you first wrote. This will allow you in review to see your own development. Later, after completing these studies, you will wish to add to your notebook or even insert a few notes in this Manual beside the printed suggestions.

Have it clearly fixed in mind, then, whenever a question is followed by a footnote number your procedure must be: (1) Put your reply in writing in your notebook. (2) Study and compare my teaching given in the answer section at the bottom of the page. (3) Continue where you left off.

Permit me to repeat. It is of utmost importance that your replies to me be nailed down in writing so that you can compare how you really think and feel with the instruction I will be giving. Keep your notebook in order by lesson number for future reference so that as you review you can see places where your understanding and attitudes have changed.

Please do not cut corners on the memory verse. Even if you are quite familiar with the assigned verse, get it down letter perfect by writing it out or reciting it to someone, stating the reference, then the verse, followed by the reference again. You should require no prompting or peeking.

Repeatedly you will encounter in the Manual the word "truth." By this is meant those precepts of God which bring us into contact with His character and into alignment with His will.

> I do not hide your righteousness in my heart; I speak of your faithfulness and salvation. I do not conceal your love and your truth from the great assembly. Do not withhold your mercy from me, O LORD; may your love and your truth always protect me. (Psalm 40:10,11).

Please enter into prayer with me now as I dedicate our time together.

> Father in heaven, you know each of our hearts. Everything in your creation is laid bare before your eyes. Open my friend's heart to your good Word. O Father, I pray that the seed will fall on good ground. Get the victory over Satan, who has caused so much defeat and hurt to us. Overcome every effort of the enemy to discourage and delay my friend in this holy exercise. O Father, get glory for yourself. Out of ashes bring forth beauty. May a new and fresh anointing of your Holy Spirit be upon us. Show us the Lord Jesus Christ as Head of a new creation and help us to live by the Holy Spirit's power in the new life you give. I do testify before You, O God of heaven, and before this new friend that you have faithfully dealt with me through many hours, and even years, of testing and struggle as I have reached for the very truths I would now share. Father, make them clear, simple, and life changing. I pray this through Jesus Christ our Lord. Amen.

Part 2

SLS Lessons

Lesson I
John 1 and 2

We open your Bible to John 1:1. **What is meant here by the term "Word"?** *1:1*

What verse in the first portion of the chapter most clearly indicates the answer to this question? If necessary, look for it.

If you do not know the answer to the first question, read verse 14 and try again.

Yes, Jesus is the very *expression* of God. Of course, a word expresses the mind of the speaker.

What would you consider to be the greatest need of an unbelieving, agnostic man? He needs to know God — that He exists and what He is like. **By what title of Jesus, then, are we shown that He meets this need?** [1]

See verse 18 were Scripture admits the impossibility of man climbing up and observing God. However, God overcomes the difficulty by coming to us.

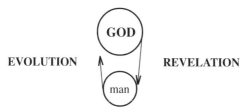

Yes, we arrive at a knowledge of the great God by His initiative, not by our evolving. It is a matter of revelation, not evolution. Further scriptures are Hebrews 1:1-3 and 1 John 1:1,2.

---

1. *As the "Word of God," Jesus brings God to us.*

1:1-3   **Where was God's son before Mary conceived and brought him to birth?** [2]

1:14   Through miraculous birth from the virgin, the Son also took on human nature. Thus this wonderful person has two natures. He is God and man, united forever. **After a man believes that God truly exists, what is his next great need?** [3] **Do you know by what title Jesus indicates that He meets that need for us?** [4]

1:29   **Why is Jesus called the Lamb of God?** [5]

As God's lamb, exactly what is Jesus here said to accomplish? How does this work? I mean, how is it that He died back there on the cross and this gets rid of my sin? Be sure to put this down in writing and remember you are not merely to affirm that Jesus does in fact gain the forgiveness of our sins. **Rather, attempt to explain how this offering of Himself actually accomplishes your forgiveness.** [6]

---

2. *This text clearly indicates that He was already in existence before the beginning of creation and was ever with the Father. He is the Creator.*

3. *To get right with God.*

4. *The Lamb of God.*

5. *Because in the Old Testament days the animals were sacrificed on the altar in payment for the sinner's debt to God.*

6. *God is angry with each sinner. We have all sinned and broken His laws. Sin is laid on the Lamb who substitutes and receives the punishment in our place. We rise and go home forgiven. God's frown turns to a smile because this is His arrangement — that the Lamb should substitute for the sinner.*

My friend, so many are vague and confused about what Jesus really accomplished. It is imperative that you see clearly that Jesus' death and resurrection provide freedom from sin's penalty and also a way of release from the power of sin.

Behind much of the confusion is the distressing fact that most Christians seem to misunderstand exactly what sin is. Now, in Scripture "sin" is used in three very distinct ways. **Attempt to list in writing the three large aspects of the subject of "sin."** [7]

Has the Lamb of God taken away your sin? All of it? **You mean you don't have any sin?** [8]

For now, let us summarize it simply. Jesus takes away sin once and for all as legal guilt. Then, there is His daily cleansing (1 John 1:9), and He helps us break sin's stranglehold on our lives.

Here are examples of true witnesses who get definite results. Notice the chain reaction. **See if you can trace all the links in the witness chain.** This same effect is evident *1:35-42* also as Philip responds to Jesus' call and then reaches out to Nathaniel. Be sure to notice the enthusiasm with which each makes his announcement about Jesus to his friend. Have you lost this note of happy enthusiasm in your witness? Have you by chance become a broken link in the chain of

---

7. *See* Special Help No. 2 *in the last chapter of this Manual.*

8. *Now you will see at once that there is a sense in which your sin is completely removed immediately. And, in another sense there is progressive release. Jesus accomplishes a twofold work: (1) Righting our wrong record in heaven. (2) Cleansing and correcting our wrong life on earth. The first refers to our legal guilt before God. Jesus died in our place, taking our punishment to remove that. The second, however, refers to the sinful defilement of heart that keeps producing our sins in word, thought, and deed.*

witness, receiving more than you have shared with others who are in desperate need?

Get a simple Gospel tract and determine to share it this coming week with a friend, asking him to report back to you his impressions. This will open an opportunity for productive discussion and witness.

2:23-25 **Do you feel these people were truly saved or not?** Think it over.

They have some kind of faith, but Jesus did not respond to them because there was something defective and deceptive about it. There is a faith which is not saving faith. **Have you ever doubted that you are truly saved?**

Some will reply, "No, never. I believe the doctrine of eternal security. Don't you? Once one is saved he can never be lost." Still others are at the far, opposite end of the confidence spectrum and they reply, "I'm so glad you asked me. I need help. I don't know where I stand with God. I know Jesus died for my sins and I believe that, but I find myself doubting my salvation again and again. It seems I simply can't find a confident trust, and without faith one cannot be saved. Is this not true?"

With which of these two responses do you most identify? Experience has shown me that the first fellow may have only a shallow, surface assurance drawn from his doctrinal angle. It has a ring of cocksureness. Whereas the second reply, though tainted with unfortunate doubt, may at least be more honest and open to assistance.

Now, before we close this first session, let me inquire again about your relationship with Christ. I don't want to take anything for granted. Are you settled and certain that you personally believe in Him? Or, maybe you have never seriously decided the issue. Read again John 1:12. Regardless of your answer to my question, kneel down now and simply as a child affirm your faith it Christ Jesus as Savior and Lord. Yield everything into His hands again. Tell Him so. Put it in definite words.

Assignment

(to be completed this week)

1. Please write down the name of the person with whom you plan to share a tract and to whom you plan to witness this week.

2. Explain to a friend or family member the three major aspects of sin. Explain also how it is that Jesus Christ takes away sin. It is very important that you give this expression. Please do it.

3. In preparation for next week, **read John 3 and 4**.

4. **Memorize John 1:12**. Get it letter perfect, saying the reference before and after the verse. Repeat it to a friend or test yourself by writing it.

Lesson II
John 3 and 4

3:1,2   Nicodemus seems to be an example of the people we looked at last week in 2:23. Jesus goes directly to this teacher's need of a new birth spiritually, verse 3.

3:16   What is God's attitude toward the world?

What two destinies are mentioned as open to man?

What is it that decides which destiny shall be ours?

In writing distinguish between believing *about* the Son and believing *in* the Son. [9]

4:6   Allow these words to paint a picture of the Lord Jesus Christ. What a sight to see!

What important truth about Jesus do you learn here? [10]

Are you perhaps a bit tired and discouraged yourself these days? Turn to Hebrews 2:18 and 4:14-16. Bow in prayer right now and thank him for coming to earth in weak human flesh. Worship him that he did not fail, and now do as verse 16 bids you. God lift your heart with new encouragement.

4:23,24   After Jesus confronted the woman with her immorality she brings up an issue which is troubling her. Jesus turns it into an opportunity for teaching.

---

9.   To believe about Jesus implies only that you agree with the facts. Whereas, believing in Him involves your personal commitment to Him as your Lord and Savior. There is no genuine faith that does not lead to obedience. See John 3:36 (NAS): "He who believes in the Son has eternal life; but he who does not obey the Son shall not see life, but the wrath of God abides on him."

10.   The realness of His human nature.

How would you define the word "Worship"? Complete in writing the following: "Worship is . . ." (Remember, these studies will lose much of their effectiveness if you do not write your answers before looking at mine.) Now, see my definition. [11]

Look at Psalm 8. Read it aloud as a worship prayer to God.

Notice that there is not a single line of request in the Psalm. It is pure worship, a giving to God. In contrast notice the opening verses of Psalms 4, 5, 6 and 7. All are petitions. Now there is nothing wrong with asking God for things. He never blames us for that. However, so many fail to worship.

It is a good experience during daily devotions [12] to take a Psalm each time, going through it and writing down all the descriptions of God you can glean from it. These will come in two ways: Sometimes you'll discover direct statements about the Lord Himself. Write down a fitting description. Secondly, you will discover certain activities performed by God. Translate these into descriptions of His character by asking, "What kind of a being is this one who can, or would, do thus and so?"

Let us now compile such a list. I have my Bible open before me at Psalm 145:8. Turn there also and make a list of descriptions of God. I will name the first one I see and you name the next and continue to alternate with me, filling in the blanks as we move through several verses.

---

11. Worship is the act of giving to God honor, glory, praise, love, adoration, thanksgiving for all that He is in Himself and also for all that He does for us, especially for giving the Lord Jesus to die for our sins.

12. See instructions for daily devotions given in this week's assignment footnote

I see first that He is gracious, _____ ,
patient, _____ , good, _____ ,
praiseworthy, _____ , glorious King,
_____ , mighty, _____ . Now
let us close there at verse 12.

There is a definite advantage to using the Psalms or some
other elevating Scripture on God in this manner. The believer's
mind and emotions are brought into a response of worship.
And, too, the will must be exercised in this holy activity.
"Through Jesus, therefore, let us continually offer to God
a sacrifice of praise — the fruit of lips that confess his
name" (Heb. 13:15). **How often do you really worship God?
How much of your prayer time is involved in Worship?**
It is important you learn to do this over an open Bible — right
from God's word.

Furthermore, if you have responsibility for a family, your
prayers at mealtime and family devotions should be marked
by elevated moments of worship and praise. Even attendance
at church should be thought of as a regular recognition of God,
a service to him.

Now, go over each aspect of your devotional life — your
private praying, family worship, church services. **How strong
and enthusiastic is praise in your life?**

Look at the seesaw sketch below and consider your own
life. [13] As a worship goes up, worry goes down. Worry tends
to dethrone God and elevate problems. Worship magnifies
God and refuses to allow molehills to become mountains. There

---

13.

26

is a certain element of pride in displacing worship. As perspective is lost, ultimate responsibilities for the future seem to be in our own hands. Ask God's pardon for failure in this area and dedicate yourself to regular employment of true worship, beginning with daily use of the Psalms in connection with your prayer time.

Once Jesus had made the dramatic revelation of himself to *4:28,29* the woman, she hurried back into the town to tell about Jesus. John mentions that she left her waterpot. Look at verse 11 and notice she had made a point of reminding Jesus that He lacked any container for the water. All is now changed for she has found living water for her heart.

Telling it is perfectly normal for one who is excited about a new relationship. "Come, see a man !" (v. 29) Here is enthusiasm.

"Many of the Samaritans from that town believed in him *4:39* because of the woman's testimony . . . ." Though she had been a very sinful person and was so new in her faith, her witness was effective. How is it with you? Did you carry out the assignment I gave you last time, to share your witness with another and give out the Gospel leaflet? You ought to do this!

"And because of his words many more became believers." *4:41* You see here that Jesus will work with you as you testify, and the Spirit will help turn people to God. The point of verse 35 is that now is the time for your testimony. People may be more ready than you think.

27

Assignment

1. Give out the tract (last week's assignment) if you have not already done so. Continue to witness.

2. Daily use the worship suggestions given this lesson. If you are not having daily personal Bible reading and prayer, see the instructions below. [14]

3. **Memorize and use in worship Rev. 15:3,4.** (Usually I assign only a single verse per week, but please learn verse 3 perfectly and at least begin verse 4.).

4. Prepare for next week by **reading John 5.**

---

14. *Every Christian needs a personal, daily meeting with God, and usually the best time is in the morning before the day's activities. This should include Bible reading and prayer. A simple, basic plan might begin with the reading of Scripture — perhaps working your way through the New Testament by taking a chapter or so each day. Note ideas for prayer as you read — whether some blessing to thank God for, or promise to claim, or sin to confess.*

Next, you might be helped in preparing for approaching God in prayer by reading a Psalm. Then with your Bible open to the place where you have meditated, kneel in prayer. Your conversation with God will generally involve three fundamental areas: 1) Worship and thanksgiving, 2) Confession of sin, 3) Requests for yourself and others, citing promises from the Word.

As time goes on, you will want to include the Old Testament in your study. When ready for it, you could begin by reading rapidly two or three chapters at a time, evenings. Generally, I would give my morning readings to the New Testament. In time, you will have a grasp of both testaments.

Lesson III
John 5

Quite a crowd must have been gathered at the feast in Jerusalem as Jesus passed through the streets. He came to one man in a crowd of needy people and knew the man's problem. For thirty-eight years he had been ailing and not able to walk. Read the text and if by any chance there is a deep need in your life, answer the Lord's question for yourself. *5:5,6*

Jesus heals the man and later returns to him with a rather sober warning, "See, you are well again. Stop sinning or something worse may happen to you." See how serious sin is. If this man returns to his old ways, something worse than thirty-eight years of paralysis will befall him! My feeling is that this man's life in the past had been marked with a serious sin failure. The warning here is the same as in John 8:11. Continuing in sin is a desperately dangerous matter. *5:14*

In the light of all this, I must ask you this important question. **Is there in your life any repeating sin over which you cannot seem to gain victory?** Take a few moments now for a sober, honest reply. I imagine that I am seated there with you and that you answer in the negative. Let us further suppose that I sense there is a bit of uncertainty in your voice and a lack of true strength in your life. In such a case, I would direct you to the same Scriptures as for the one in admitted defeat. So, regardless of your answer, it might be well to make a thoughtful inspection of some important Scriptures. Please turn to Galatians 5:19-21. Take your notebook and **attempt to categorize the several types of sins represented in the Apostle's listing.** For this study, I recommend use of a translation more modern than the King James, like the New American Standard or the New International Version.

You will notice that Paul places related terms together in four different groups. For example, look at verse 19. **All these terms represent what kind of sin?** [15]

Can you discover and label the Apostle's remaining three groups? [16]

Notice the extremely serious warning that follows, "Those who live like this will not inherit the Kingdom of God."

Go over your life carefully in the light of each of these fundamental categories of sin. **In which are you most likely to fail?** You might also profit from studying Ephesians 5:3-6. You will find some of the same terms again, with one additional basic sin — covetousness. This represents man's selfish relationship with the entire material world. It is a large, fundamental category of sin and should be added to the other listing. Notice again the warning is given that no such person "has any inheritance in the kingdom of Christ and of God. Let no one deceive you with empty words, for because of such things God's wrath comes on those who are disobedient." (Eph. 5:5,6).

First Corinthians 6:9-20 ought also to be studied at this point.

What God is saying is crystal clear: you cannot both choose sin and choose me. You must give up claim to one or the other relationship. Do not be deceived into thinking that you can willfully walk the broad road and yet end up in heaven. It is the narrow road of self-surrender that leads to life.

---

15. Sexual sins.

16. Idolatry and witchcraft come next in verse 20. These might be labeled as wrong expressions of religion. Then follows a long list of attitude sins, that are shown in relationship with others. The last two terms there in verse 21 might be labeled sins of indulgence and appetites.

If you are one who has been struggling with the burden of habitual sin, admit it, identify it by its proper name, then have a showdown with God in prayer. I will help you do it now. I suggest you kneel for this important prayer with the Manual open before you. In your own words using a strong voice, follow these steps:

1. Admit the sins or sin by name to God.

2. Thank God for the blood of Jesus Christ which cleanses the sins you have named. Read aloud 1 John 1:7.

3. Acknowledge Jesus Christ as Lord and Master of all. Now present everything to Him — your stubborn will, troubled emotions, ambitions, mind, abilities, every faculty and even your physical body — its members, desires and ailments. Make the dedication of Romans 12:1, 2.

4. Take a definite, strong stand in the authority of the Lord Jesus Christ — the One you have just named as Lord over you. Use words of strength, such as: "Lord, I choose your way." Or, "I believe your Word." Or, "I thank you that . . . ." If there is an intense struggle with Satan, take your stand definitely using such terms as: "I refuse to believe the lies of my enemy." Or, "I reject this mood of despair." Or even, "In the name of the Lord Jesus Christ, I order you, Satan, out!" Here you will need to read and affirm each truth taught in Colossians 1:13,14. Notice that two opposing authorities are mentioned and thank God you are transferred and brought under the authority of the beloved Son. This wonderful transaction is accomplished by the blood redemption. Praise God!

5. Turn to thanksgiving, praising God item by item for many of His good deeds toward you. Mention carefully the works of the Son. God's care as Father. The patient ministries of the Holy Spirit sustaining and comforting you. Your family and material benefits, and other things. Do not

31

look back into the swamp. Look up to God. And if necessary, again go over the Scripture used, praising God openly and definitely for each good truth.

6. Ask that you might be refreshed, filled and restored by the Holy spirit.

As often as old doubts and temptations recur, use the same prayer, beginning with thanksgiving that the blood of Christ has indeed paid for each named sin. Then move down the steps of the prayer as I have listed them. Thus, it will become a battle prayer for you and you will be on the aggression. Copy the steps and Scriptures down on the paper right now. Keep a copy with you over the next days. Use as often as you begin to feel rattled, even if it means twenty times a day. Don't be a sitting duck. Keep on the move. Stay in charge of your life in Christ's name. It works. We are more than conquerors! (Romans 8:37)

One final word: Have written out, or better yet, memorize 1 John 1:7 and Colossians 1:13,14 so you can use them at a moment's notice in your praying. Another simple verse filled with power is John 8:36. Lay hold of that also and may God make you free indeed.

5:18-29 Here we breathe a bit of Heaven's air as we pray down through the truths about Christ set forth in these verses:

Equal with God (18)

Author of our spiritual life (24-26)

Judge of all (27) one day opening the graves and dividing forever among men. (See *Special Help No. 3.*)

5:39 **According to this one verse, what would you say is the grand focal point of all Scripture?** [17]

Look up 2 Timothy 3:16. "Inspiration" means "God-breathed." Words of Scriptures are breathed by God through

---

17. *Jesus Christ. "Scriptures testify of me," He says.*

the pen of his chosen writers. They wrote the Word, it is clear, but God saw to it that they wrote what He wanted written. 2 Peter 1:21 shows us how God used these holy writers for this high purpose. Scripture may accurately be said to be the very Word of God. Or, returning to our text in John 5:39, the Bible is God's official testimony of His Son. What a serious thing to shut off God's communication! Leaving your Bible closed does exactly that!

Where are you now on your daily reading? Be definite with me in your answer. I'm not asking you whether you sometimes open the Bible here or there — perhaps in the Psalms — for brief reading. If you do not regularly read, I suggest you face it for what it is — a sinful neglect of the Lord Himself. Make things right with God now in prayer.

Surely, a growing Christian needs more than a mini-diet of canned devotional food. You need to have your own plan of searching through Scripture and feeding your heart. Let me repeat and expand a bit on what I suggested in last week's assignment. Read consecutively through a book. That is the way Scripture is written. Think of each book as God's letter to you. If you are quite out of touch with him, as far as regular Bible reading goes, then I suggest you begin at the simplest book — Mark's Gospel. Take only a chapter or section a day at first. Complete it and jot on a piece of paper some encouraging insight you wish to claim for yourself. Perhaps the Spirit will also bring to mind some sin or weakness you need to turn from or guard against. Also, look for something praiseworthy about God you can mention to Him in worship. Do this in prayer. At last, the healing flow of God's Word will again be moving through your life. As you become able to take more nourishment, I would encourage a solid, regular morning appointment with God before you get into the day. Read straight through the New Testament, taking a chapter or two each morning. Then as you go to prayer read one of the praise Psalms to get your mind and heart functioning in a prayerful attitude. Be sure you make full use of these Scriptures to prepare for genuine worship. During the day, try to recollect key truths you gleaned from your morning devotional time. At night, try rapid reading directly through the Old Testament. Do it for the sheer pleasure and the knowledge you will glean by skim-reading [18] quickly through the books. Do not feel guilty if you miss a few things. Keep moving and seek an overview. Later, you can gain a fuller mastery of the details. Don't drown yourself in discouragement trying to get everything at once.

---

18. *Skim-reading or rapid-reading means that you would move more quickly over the chapters without stopping to study them. You would rather read simply for the profit and enjoyment of the story or lesson, feeling free to skip material that is more difficult.*

Assignment

1. As you guard against evils mentioned in Galatians 5:19-21, give attention to the positive good fruit of the Spirit and verses 22 and 23. Which of these are in cultivation in your life? Thank God for it in prayer.
2. **Read Chapters 6 and 7 of John.**
3. Determine what the hungering and thirsting stand for in John 6:35.
4. How would you answer the question asked by the Jews in John 7:15?
5. **Memory verse: 1 Corinthians 10:13.** Remember, it must be letter perfect with the reference recited before and after the verse. Also, finish **memorizing Revelation 15:3,4.** Writing the verses from memory will be most helpful.

Lesson IV
John 6 and 7

6:9 How inadequate seemed the few loaves and small fish! **Do you at times feel that way about your own abilities and spiritual resources?** "How far will they go among so many?"

Just as Christ took this inadequate supply, blessed and multiplied it, so He can do with us. He can use what we have and multiply it. This might be a good time to dust the cellar windows in your life, open the doors, and let in a little sunshine and fresh air. (Study *Special Help No. 4.*)

6:35 Look back at your completed assigment in preparation for this session. **What do the figures of speech "hunger" and "thirst" represent?** Jesus is obviously speaking of more than barely being saved. Jesus is here offering satisfaction. The hungering and thirsting are terms used to indicate a sense of unmet need. Jesus Christ completes the unfulfilled life. He meets inner longings and supplies the empty areas with fulness.

Whether it is a need for companionship, a struggle for spiritual growth, or some other legitimate desire, the Lord Jesus Christ can meet it. He will either fill in with a new presense of Himself or give a practical, providential answer. In addition, He can silence those carnal demands and longings that are not legitimate.

6:37,44 Assurance is again given that, once we are His, He truly keeps us. We did not gain acceptance by our own effort, nor are we dependent on self-help for our security. Indeed, believers are the Father's gift to the Son and He does not cast aside such a treasure.

6:47-58 Notice the eating and drinking exactly parallels believing. This word figure of intimately taking Christ into our lives

36

is aimed at emphasizing that the Redeemer's life becomes ours. We live by Him even as He on earth lived by the Father (v. 57).

No hiding sin! Jesus knows about it and He knows ahead *6:64,70* of time.

Jesus explains why divisions inevitably come between *7:7* Him and the wicked world around. **What is the reason?** Beginning with this chapter (see vv. 12 and 43), this section of John will emphasize the intense divisions which Jesus' life and ministry brought.

Because of your life in Christ, has anyone separated from you? Are there tensions anywhere — at home, school, where you work or live? If these difficulties are truly because of Christ and not your own failures, then rejoice because you are right on schedule! Beware of an overshadowing discouragement because of this. Many evils grow in the shadows of despondency. To regain lost perspective, read Matthew 10:28-39. If you happen to be married to an unbelieving partner, a new look at 1 Corinthians 7:12-16 might encourage you at this point.

What is your answer to the Jews question? (See also v. *7:15* 46.) I hope you have something written down from your assignment. Notice Jesus answers the question in the next verse, explaining that the wise teachings are from the Father. This looks deeply into the realness of Christ's humanity. He came and served as a Spirit-filled man, the Holy Spirit being given Him without measure (John 3:34). Of course, Jesus is true deity. The Second Person of the Trinity. He did not cease being God while on earth. Study carefully and thoughtfully Acts 10:38; 2:22 and John 14:10.

You'll see that Jesus really places Himself in the same league with us. Though He is ever omnipotent (all-powerful), He performs His work as a Spirit-filled man. Though He is omnipresent (present everywhere), when He desires to get across town, He walks. By the power the Spirit, He discerns the thoughts of His enemies.

Peter, as well as Jesus, raised the dead. So be careful how you argue from miraculous works of Jesus to His deity. The best line of argumentation would run this way: Jesus' powerful works and wisdom in teaching show He is truly God's man, filled with the Spirit as none other. You can trust a God-filled man. This One says, "I am the Son of God." He is very God, the Son. Amen.

Remember, do not view Jesus' life as one blazing ball of glory from the Second Person of the Trinity. Except for the Mount of Transfiguration, He was seen as a humble man in touch with us, even promising greater works to His followers (14:12). But His miracles and godly life certified His teachings, which make clear He is the very Son of God. The content of our knowledge of His divine Person comes from His doctrine, not simply from the signs.

7:37-39   Take your notebook and answer this series of questions in writing from the text:

What is the drink spoken of here?

Where must you go to obtain this ?

What is it that brings us to Christ for this?

Make sure you have each answer in your notebook before proceeding.

The first question is answered in 7:39. The Holy Spirit is this precious drink which we so desperately need. Jesus alone is the fountain for this filling. Unless Jesus is given His place of honor at the right hand of God, when we seek the Holy Spirit we may be deceived and have a false experience. Study Acts 2:32,33. You will see it simply diagrammed on the next page.

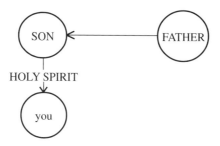

The Son as Mediator is shown here elevated to the right hand of the Father. There He receives the Holy Spirit from the Father and shares Him with us. This is the "divine route" of the Spirit. Make sure you stand where the showers are real. The Lord Jesus Christ must be in His place.

Returning to John 7, look at verses 38 and 39. **Attempt to list on paper the sequence of events indicated there. Put them in some kind of chronological order.** See if you can do it yourself on paper. (Hint: Begin at the end and work somewhat backward.) [19]

Is this divine plan at work in your life?

Understanding the baptism of the Spirit is very important. The gentle presence of the Spirit was symbolized by a dove, visibly coming "down from heaven" and remaining on Jesus at His baptism in the river (John 1:32, 33). "For the one whom God has sent speaks the words of God, for God gives the Spirit without limit" (John 3:34). Thus, Jesus is for us the inexhaustible source of the Holy Spirit. He is the One "who will baptize with the Holy Spirit." Romans 6:3-5

---

19. It all began when Jesus was raised from the dead and glorified at God's right hand. This set everything in motion. Here then is the order: (1) Jesus glorified. (2) The general giving of the Spirit (Pentecost). (3) Believing by individuals. (4) Personal reception of the Spirit by each one who believes. (5) Outflow of the Spirit's blessing from the believer to others.

teaches us that it is by means of the Spirit's baptism, symbolized by our water baptism, that we are united with Christ in a twofold manner:

(1) God counts us in Jesus when he died for our sins. Through the Spirit's work we are brought into our Lord's very body and are counted as having died with Him. Thus, we are released from any further legal threat (Romans 6:7).

(2) Now this baptismal union extends also to the new life we have with the resurrected Lord. Read the following verses in that same section of Romans and rejoice. How good is it to be incorporated into our Lord and also to be part of His body of believers! (1 Corinthians 12:13)

Assignment

1. Notice various tests that stretch and challenge your faith this week. Make a written note of each one and indicate how you responded to Jesus Christ who works in all these things. Remember, too, that faith and obedience need each other. What did you learn from these tests? Note again John 7:37.
2. Now look at John 7:38 and strive for an outflow this week.
3. Prepare for next session by **reading John 8 in 9**.
4. **Memory verse: Acts 1:8**.

Lesson V
John 8 and 9

Why is it so important to have a correct understanding *8:23,24*
about Jesus? Be sure you get your answer from the text
itself. [20]

Let no one ever say it does not matter if people have
differing views about our Lord's Person. One's eternal destiny
hangs upon this great doctrine. Did the Son of God exist
before His birth on that first Christmas? Yes! (See verse
23 and the discussion in verses leading up to 58. Read
again John 1:1-3.)

Here is a good life rule. See also Colossians 3:17. **Do** *8:29*
you avoid even questionable things? (Check *Special*
Helps No. 4 on "Questionable Things.")

Notice all the steps covered in these verses, leading up to *8:30-32*
the last word in 32, which is the word "free." **List them.** [21]

Have you come to this greater freedom? Only through a
more real and true knowing of God's Word is it possible.
Have you daily read God's Word, following the plan we
established in Lesson 3?

What does it mean to be "free"? [22] *8:33-36*

Again, permit me to ask, have you the freedom described
in the footnote? **In what ways as a Christian are you**

---

20. *Without a correct belief in Jesus, one perishes in sin.*

21. *He speaks the word, many believe, the believers are
ordered to continue in His word. Then they become true disciples.
These come to know the truth and finally the truth releases them
to a greater freedom.*

22. *The right to choose. At liberty to determine and to follow
through with desired action. Ability to function without
restraining hindrances.*

41

not free? Consider anger, self-pity, pride, fear, doubt, feelings of inferiority, bitterness, dread of failure. You see, sins in attitude or character as well as overt, evil deeds are serious in God's eyes.

Now, read again 8:34. **Define this bondage.** Not only is there inability to do the desired good service to God, but also there is the compulsion to do wrong. The sin-slave is held in service to evil promptings. Roots from a wrong nature bring forth fruit and distort points of view, establishing wrong habits, appetites, and attitudes.

Happily, the Son Himself stands ready to bring freedom (v. 36). If you have a need in this regard, turn back to the showdown prayer given in the section on John 5:14. Use that right now.

Notice again verse 32, remembering that the Word of God is a great means in your liberation. You must use it continually. There is no way to remain free without its regular employment. The only answer to the dark is light. "Your word is a lamp to my feet and a light for my path" (Psalm 119:105). Remember also to continue use of the prayer outline in daily "battle praying."

8:42-47 Perhaps you have heard one ask upon reading the daily news, what makes people act as they do? **Answer the question from this section of John.**

You will see Jesus traces it to one's roots. Our spiritual parentage traces back to God or to Satan. We are thus said to be either of God or of the devil. And we act accordingly. This interesting line of truth is brought out also in John's first epistle (1 John 3 and 4). Actions, therefore, trace back to character and our character has deep spiritual roots.

8:56-59 Here Jesus plainly asserts the great doctrine of his pre-existence. "I always AM," he says in effect. It is clear that they understand Him to be asserting his deity. That is why they instantly respond with stones just as they did previously in 5:18.

For a little refresher of history, and so you will get the impact of the discussion, try to recall how far back Abraham lived before Jesus' day. **How many years?** [23]

Now, draw a time line. At one end put a stick figure representing Abraham. At the other end write the word NOW, representing our present age and time. Your time line, then, will be 4,000 years in length. Place a cross exactly midway between the two points, representing Jesus' time, and you will see that Abraham lived approximately as far back in into BC as we are in AD. Copy my time line example into your notebook and then attempt to complete it as I will direct. [24]

Roughly, who lived midway between Abraham and Jesus? Make another mark at the 1,000 BC point and write his name. What famous Old Testament character would then appear on your chart midway between Abraham and your newest addition, that is, about 1,500? (Rough approximation.) Finally, put a mark at the 500 BC point and indicate what event was taking place at that time. [25]

---

23. 2000 years BC

24.

25. To complete your time line chart you will need: King David, and before him, Moses, and finally, the Jews returning from exile.

43

It is extremely important that every Bible student have firmly fixed in his mind a simple, basic outline of Old Testament history. Without such an outline in mind, the Old Testament will not "hang together" as you read it. It is tragic that after years of Bible reading many believers are left with a kind of devotional mush because they have no framework or skeleton on which to hang the truths as they read.

Open your Bible to the very front and study the Table of Contents. The sixty-six books in the sacred collection are in an orderly arrangement. The Old Testament is before Christ. Putting it very, very simply, the first seventeen books tell the story of God's making the world and His plan of redemption from sin. He chooses the Hebrew people and establishes them in Palestine. Their kingdom falls and finally they struggle back from exile. The five middle books are poetry and wisdom, written by those who lived during the Old Testament period of history. The final seventeen Old Testament books are writings of the prophets who ministered during the same period covered by the first seventeen books. After the Old Testament age, four hundred years pass in silence. Then the New Testament takes up the story with the four books or Gospels on Jesus' life, and continues with the acts of His followers (Acts) as they established the church. These workman also penned the letters which follow. Note that all Paul's epistles are together. Revelation is a fitting climax to God's Word. All this is simplified, I know, but at least it will prove that the layout of Scripture is really no impossible puzzle and the Bible ought not to be thought of as scrambled by an egg beater.

9:1-3   Why this affliction? The disciples want to know. All this need answers to this question, both for our own peace of mind and in order to encourage others who are fainting under their difficulties.

Why all the suffering in the world? There is no one answer, but **make a list of the various possible explanations for the afflictions and sufferings men endure.** After doing so, check yours against my list which follows.

1. A judgmental stroke from God. The disciples were wrong in supposing this to be the case with the blind man. However, there are those who suffer in this way. Such was the case with those who brought judgment on themselves for partaking of the Lord's table in an unworthy manner (1 Corinthians 11:20, 30). Apparently some of them had even died under this punishment. In no sense was that judgment of a corrective nature. Perhaps this is what was warned of in John 5:14, also.

2. General calamities such as those mentioned in the opening portion of Luke 13. These seem to prove nothing more than the general humiliation of man's fallen condition. Some died under the outburst of a tyrant. Others perished under the catastrophe of a falling tower.

3. Satan's assaults. Luke 13:16 makes it clear this was the case with the stooped woman. In addition, there are other bruisings which come even to faithful Christians in spiritual warfare.

4. Chastisement and correction, such as mentioned in Hebrews 12:5.

5. Trial and strengthening of faith as covered in 1 Peter.

6. Suffering for the display of God's works. This was the case in our text. God uses such experiences in two ways: (1) To sustain his child in the test, displaying his enabling grace, as with the Apostle Paul in 2 Corinthians 12. Or, (2) Showing His delivering power, as with the blind man in John 9.

9:4   Brevity of time makes our work for God urgent. It is so important that the gospel story of Jesus reach people who need it.

9:25   **Do you ever hold back from testifying of the Lord because you feel a lack of experience, ability, or knowledge?** Then, remember the example of this man whom Jesus healed. He knew so little and yet he spoke what he knew. That is all God expects from you.

9:34-38   True enough, his testimony was rejected, but Jesus came along directly to strengthen him with a more complete revelation of himself. See it in the dramatic and touching account here. Could it be that Jesus is withholding further insights from you or me simply because we have not practiced sharing what we do know?

9:20-22   Before leaving this incident, it might be helpful if we notice the behavior of the blind man's parents. They withheld needed support to him. Too many parents fail to sense deeply the pressures upon their children. Indeed, all spiritually young need sensitive care and encouragement. **Do you know of a new Christian you might encourage? In what ways?**

Assignment

1. Think this week about simply living so as to please God. Note any changes in attitude, actions or decisions you make because of this axiom in John 8:29.
2. **Read John 10 and 11.**
3. **Memorize Colossians 1:13.**

Lesson VI
John 10 and 11

10:1-18   Learning to get exactly what we need from God's Word is an important skill. Here is an excellent text to use in practice. Though familiar, it is filled with good things. **Go down the verses and make a list of all the provisions which our dear Shepherd offers us.** See how many you can find, either stated directly or implied.

Write down a troubling situation you are now facing, or an area of your life where there is a struggle. Then, turn to your list and choose the provision that would meet this particular need. Bow in prayer and thankfully claim it for your life.

Be sure to notice all the opposition facing the poor sheep: the stranger whose unfamiliar voice causes the sheep to flee from him (4, 5). Thieves and robbers (8, 10). They come to steal, kill and destroy. The sheep refuse them and cling to the Shepherd who gives abundant life. The hireling forsakes the sheep as the wolf approaches (12, 13). The pitiable flock is invaded and scattered. But above all this, see the picture the faithful Shepherd, willing to lay down His life for His flock.

Woven into this account is the idea that the sheep ought to distinguish their Shepherd's voice from any other. Furthermore, their very weakness causes them to cling to him.

Behind all these attacks on God's flock is the great enemy Satan. More frequent than violent persecution is the misleading voice. Do you recognize it?

At this point, you should not only be thinking of false teachings about God; what of distortions about others and yourself as well? There is something about our sinful nature that readily echoes in response to Satan's subtle voice. His transmissions are intended to distress and disturb emotions, the mind, the will, and even the physical body.

Go down this list and see how many of these attitudes you frequently express, at least inwardly:

1. "I'm only human — nobody's perfect."
2. "I can't."
3. "I'm so weak."
4. "I'm simply letting the Lord lead — just letting go and letting God."
5. "I know so little in comparison to others."

With which ones do you identify? Now compare each of these "inner voices" with this list of thoughtful evaluations:

1. Sounds like an excuse for sins.
2. Frequently a cover for "I won't."
3. A deception if there is resistance to God's offer of gracious help.
4. Sometimes this indicates an irresponsible passivity with an element of rebellion or refusal to obey actively.
5. Very bad, if coupled with a stubborn refusal to move ahead in knowing God and his word. Men know channel and time of their favorite TV program because they are that interested. Chapter and verse of God's promises may also be learned by God's people. Remember God's complaint against sinners: "There is no one who understands, no one who seeks God." (Rom. 3:11).

Many Christians tend to one extreme or the other regarding the devil. Either, they ignore and forget him. Or else, they are preoccupied with thoughts of demons. I do not intend to promote an unhealthy involvement with the satanic. On the other hand, the mass of Scripture on the

49

devil and his subtleties must be faced. We are ordered to wrestle and resist, to be watchful and not to be ignorant of his devices. **Are you obeying these commands?**

For further instruction regarding the devil, see *Special Help No. 5.*

10:19-21   Again divisions come up because of Jesus Christ. Such pressures prove the realness of our faith. Study 1 John 3:1 and 2 Corinthians 6:14-7:1.

10:28-30   Blessed security! **How do you answer the objection that this passage seems to allow one to sin as much as he might wish and yet feel secure and safe?** [26]

11:1-6   Jesus' special friend Lazarus is desperately ill, struggling for his life. On purpose, Jesus stays away two more days until He can announce to his disciples, "Lazarus is dead." The anguish of the situation and Jesus' lack of response leaves the disciples and Martha and Mary bewildered and floundering in the quandaries. **Go through the chapter and**

---

26. *There two good answers, both in verse 27. (Always get an answer from the immediate context whenever possible.) First, the nature of the good Shepherd's sheep is to hear His voice and follow Him. Believers, therefore, have a new nature which simply will not continually resist the Spirit's leading (Romans 8:14). Secondly, verse 27 also suggests that the very nature of the Shepherd's care over us means that He knows His sheep and takes care of them. If they are without His care, and that includes the needed chastening, they are none of His (Hebrews 12:8). Thus, one who is without evidence of a new nature or the great Shepherd's care may not be called "saved" with any degree of certainty. We see, therefore that the nature of God's work within each believer and also His watchfulness over them prevent the abuse of these precious verses. Study Philippians 1:6.*

pick out verses which offer keys of release for you when dark questionings arise. [27]

Jesus as a true man shared the burden of His friends. *11:35* Remember again Hebrews 2:17, 18 and John 4:6. Now they are about to see a mighty demonstration of His power over death. See John 5:21-29.

What a prayer relation existed between Jesus and his *11:41-42* Father! Martha's confidence in Jesus' prayers was strong at first, then wavered a bit. Compare verse 22 with 39.

To get the full impact of our Lord's confidence, you have to picture him standing there before the uncovered tomb wherein lies a body, dead for four days. Hear Him now as He looks toward heaven and prays, "Father, I thank you that you have heard me. I knew that you always hear me, but I said this for the benefit of the people standing here, that they may believe that you sent me."

Apparently, then, this prayer is made public in order for you and me to learn something from it. Taken wrongly, it might be such a high example that you and I would be discouraged into complaining, "This is beyond my capabilities in prayer!" However, there is a very important lesson for us here. Allow me ask you now: **If I truly pray in Jesus' name, what assurance do these verses 41 and**

---

27. Verses 4, 15, 25, 26, 40, 42. Studying these verses will enable you to understand how Jesus could both love his friends (v. 5) and yet be glad they were left to face their dark predicament (v. 15). Sometimes it hurts us to be stretched but it is worth it when God is glorified and our faith is enlarged. Remember, there is no trial that is not a trial! Here is a good point for you to approach God in prayer and tell Him that you accept any testing that you may be enduring. Now thank Him for it and ask that His purposes be fully realized.

42 give me? After you have put your answer in writing, proceed.

The secret of prevailing prayer is to pray in Jesus' name. You see, He is always heard by His Father. That is the grand truth being revealed to us here. We are given insight into the very relationship between the Father and His Son, and we learn that the Father always, without exception, grants the requests of Jesus. This means that when I pray in Jesus' name, I am simply approaching the Father on the basis of that glorius relationship between God and Jesus.

Putting it a bit crudely, let me ask: Do you know how to cash in on this glorious relationship between the Father and His Son, Jesus? You do so by standing in Jesus Christ. By praying in His name. **Exactly how does one do that?** Attempt to set that down in writing now. Remember, you are answering the question, "How?" Write it before reading further.

Obviously, this requires more than just saying the words at prayer's end, "In Jesus' name, Amen." It means to begin and continue the entire prayer on the basis of the merit of Jesus Christ in the eyes of the Father. He is a Son well-pleasing to His Father. This might be more real to the eye of your faith if frequently you begin your prayer with such words as "Father, I come to You now through your Son Jesus Christ," or, "In the name of Jesus Christ I stand before You now." Sometimes, begin with a statement of our Lord's blood atonement for you. Then go on to say that it is because of His righteousness you now appear in the Father's presense with your worship and petitions. Prayer truly offered in His name will not be denied.

Perhaps one of the important keys to all Scripture is understanding how God is now reconciled toward us, that is, turned again with a receiving smile toward man because of His satisfaction with His own son. We, then, stand in Him and are also received, answered, blessed. Actually, the great promises of Scripture, then, are made specially to the well-pleasing Son, not directly to us. It is only as we line up ourselves with God by standing in Jesus' name that we are certain of the answer. This is how we obtain all promises.

For example, look at Isaiah 50:4. **Is that promise available to you?** Suppose in a testimony meeting a humble woman rises to her feet and says, "God promises in Isaiah 50:4 to give me 'an instructed tongue, to know the word that sustains the weary'; therefore, I am claiming this tomorrow as I speak with my neighbor." You will see by studying the context that these words are addressed to the Messiah, but the promise is ours in Him. The great secret we are striving to learn is exactly this: How to claim the good things that God is now willing to pour out upon men as they approach Him in Jesus' name. Shape your praying by this truth. For, "All things are yours, whether . . . the world or life or death or the present or the future — all are yours, and you are of Christ, and Christ is of God" (1 Cor. 3:21-23). "For no matter how many promises God has made, they are 'Yes' in Christ. And so through Him the 'Amen' is spoken by us to the glory of God" (2 Cor. 1:20).

Assignment

1. Begin a more definite practice of praying truly in Jesus' name. Plan the manner in which you will enter God's presence, and state very definitely your position in Christ as you begin your prayer. Do this carefully each time you pray.

2. Mark other truths in this week's lesson that you should remember and work into your life.

3. Read for next session **John 12 and 13**.

4. **Memorise Romans 12:1**.

Lesson VII
John 12 and 13

A strong call to give ourselves over to Jesus Christ without holding back is now before us. Yielding to God is a large theme in this chapter of John. *12:1-8*

Refresh yourself with Mary's example. Without reservation, she poured out precious ointment upon Jesus and humbly, lovingly washed His feet with her hair. Apparently, the monetary value of this Eastern treasure was nearly a year's wages. There was no holding back. She broke open and emptied it for Jesus' sake.

Such a sacrifice of love affects others. "And the house was filled with the fragrance of the perfume." First of all, Jesus Himself was honored and encouraged by the offering. So large was the value of the ointment, Judas was aggravated by it. But, for those whose hearts were in tune with Christ, there was a sobering sweetness to it all.

> I will extol the LORD at all times;
> his praise will always be on my lips.
> My soul will boast in the LORD;
> let the afflicted hear and rejoice.
> Glorify the LORD with me;
> let us exalt his name together. (Psalm 34:1-3)

With this scene before you, make a one-sentence evaluation in your notebook of your sacrifice for Jesus Christ in each of following areas: worship, money, time, actual effort in serving. The saying is true that we can give without loving, but we cannot love without giving.

Next we come to our Lord's own example of giving. Verse 24 takes us into the garden where a seed is about to die. A choice is before it. If the tiny kernel is kept back from the *12:23-33*

55

soil, it will be preserved. It might even be enclosed in plastic and placed on a desk, or perhaps become a shiney ornament, but it will in such a case remain forever alone. If that seed, however, experiences a dying in the ground, it will presently arise from the mud, and flower into much fruit. This the choice Christ was to make. And, it is His call to us. Will you keep your life only for selfish purposes? Or, will you invest it in a kind of death-sacrifice for God and others?

Noticing again the qualifying "if" — "if it dies" — that is the requirement for a life that brings much fruit. Take your paper and put it down in writing — **What is this death Jesus is requiring of you?** Incidentally, the next verse makes it plain that He expects us to follow Him to the cross. But, **exactly what is involved in this dying? Give examples in writing.** [28]

> Then he called the crowd to him along with his disciples and said: "If anyone would come after me, he must deny himself and take up his cross and follow me. For whoever wants to save his life will lose it, but whoever loses his life for me and for the gospel will save it. (Mark 8:34,35)

---

28. (1) Maintaining a yielded, humble disposition. Willingness to say, I am wrong. Down must go all pride! (2) Financial adjustment, as you share offerings at church and help friends in need. (3) Maybe taking a lesser job to allow more time for God, rather than a career which consumes your time, energies and interests. (4) Interruptions of schedule and time. (5) Drain on personal inner resources as you attempt to help others. (6) If yours is a singular call into Christian service, it might well mean a costly reshaping of your entire life program. (7) In a word, self-denial.

The larger context of these interesting verses makes clear that the time referred to when He uses the word "now" is that of His upcoming crucifixion. It will be an occasion of judgment, of the overthrow of Satan, and of calling men to be saved. **What does that expression mean, "now the prince of this world will be driven out"? Who is the prince of the world? Is the devil really overthrown or not?** It seems he is on a world-wide rampage, working as never before. **What then is our text saying?** [29]

It is all quite true that we may see the devil going about today seeking whom he may devour. However, the authority of Jesus Christ has now been established by His cross. All is committed justly into His hand. The devil is defrocked of his right and unless Christians yield over to him their wills or areas of responsibility, Satan cannot exercise any claim on them. However, this does not mean that we might not yield up our rights. By much deception, he attempts to lead us to leave areas of our lives unguarded or he harasses us with guilty feelings. However, Revelation 12:11 makes it clear that God values the blood of Christ and thereby sets us free as we claim it in prayer and testimony. "They overcame him by the blood of the Lamb and by the word of their testimony; they did not love their lives so much as to shrink from death." Refresh yourself just now by making this claim in definite prayer.

---

29. *By the sacrifice of Jesus on the cross, sin is paid for. Sinners though we may be, mankind is not abandoned en masse by God. Satan's jurisdiction is completely broken off from the people of God. Indeed, the die is cast and he will ultimately be thrown into the lake of fire, with all his hosts. Satan's overthrow is essentially in the area of rights and privileges. He is absolutely without independent authority over the child of God.*

Remember that a part of our spiritual discipline is that we wrestle against the devil by claiming our spiritual privilege and place in Jesus Christ. If one goes in the ring with a champion he will be defeated, unless he wrestles intelligently and actively. "Submit yourselves, then, to God. Resist the devil, and he will flee from you" (James 4:7).

Wholesome worship of our exalted Lord does much to keep the Christian in freedom. Use such passages as Ephesians 1:20-23 and 1 Peter 3:22. Make your own list of texts but place Jesus in top authority.

To bring all this more into focus, see how Jesus uses the words "authority" and "power" in teaching his disciples: "I have given you authority . . . to overcome all the power of the enemy . . ." (Luke 10:19). Though Satan has awesome power, believers have authority. The enemy, therefore, has no right to exercise control over Christians. However, by default, neglect, and passivity the believer may fail to exercise his privileges in Christ and subject himself needlessly to the enemy. On the other hand, when we stand in the name of Jesus Christ and resist the devil, our enemy knows that back of us is Jesus the Lord. Amen.

12:42,43 **From whom do you most desire praise?** There is an inevitable choice before each one of us. (See John 5:44.) One seeks the honor of his message-source. "He who speaks on his own does so to gain honor for himself, but he who works for the honor of the one who sent him is a man of truth; there is nothing false about him" (John 7:18). Be careful here. A self-centered person organizes his values and doctrines about his own ambitions, desires, and appetites. He propounds the teachings and principles that support these. "He wants to please his commanding officer" (2 Tim. 2:4).

13:1-5 From heaven to the feet of men, the One who supplied the vast ocean basins now fills the washbasin and cleanses the feet of his disciples. Verses 12-17 make it clear that He intends this example to be followed by us. **List several examples of humble, personal service the Lord might want from you.**

Notice further that happiness might be dependent upon our response to Jesus' call here (verse 17). Study also Luke 22:24-27 and John 13:34, 35.

Peter was not at first receptive to Jesus' ministry. In the *13:6-11* family of God when one gives, another must receive. Pride is critically damaging when it makes us resistant to the Lord Himself. **What is the meaning of verse 10?** "Jesus answered, 'A person who has had a bath needs only to wash his feet; his whole body is clean . . . .' "

I picture a man there in the ancient East who has just dressed following a refreshing bath. He takes a brief walk in the evening and, returning home, kicks off his open sandals and cleanses his feet from a bit of dust. Now he's completely clean again. So it is that one who has had the full bath of personal salvation needs only to have the daily cleansing from life's stains and he remains clean and fresh before God.

When should we confess our sins to God? Suppose you ask a friend that question and he explains how he sets aside a time of quiet each night before retiring for making right the day's wrongs and confessing any sin to the Lord. Now what comment should you give?

Obviously, sin should be confessed at once. We should not carry the clutter and defilement of failure throughout the day. Even when we cannot get alone and kneel in quietness, still will to confess sin directly with an immediate cry to God (1 John 1:9-2:2).

Now we understand what was in the deep background of *13:2* Matthew 26:14-16. Next, things got even worse. Read John 13:27. When inner deception becomes a settled, established pattern, Satan always increases his hold on the

59

life. We cannot safely allow him leverage. In Judas' case the devil was simply claiming what was really his own.

It is important that we establish our line of defense in our mind and in our attitudes. Does your inner life display the freedom Christ brings?

Assignment

1. Make a daily record of your responses to the major lessons of this session. Jot down in writing the answers to these questions as you go through each day:
   (1) Has the fragrance of my worship gladdened the Lord's heart today?
   (2) Examples today of dying in order to produce "fruit." (Counting for God at some cost to me.)
   (3) Evidences of warfare against Satan.
   (4) Opportunities for "washing feet" and serving others.
2. In preparation for next session, **read John 14 and 15.**
3. **Memory verse: Romans 12:1,2.**

Lesson VIII
John 14 and 15

Before opening the Scripture, let me ask: **Where is Jesus right now? What do you picture Him doing?** Put your answer in writing. My answer will be seen shortly with still more to be added in next week's session.

14:12 Can it be that we or any of the Lord's disciples perform greater works than Christ? That is what the verse is saying. Stop and think for a moment. Jesus preached in Jerusalem and they killed Him. Peter preached there and thousands repented. **Now, in what sense do these greater works depend upon the absence of the Lord as our text suggests?** [30]

14:13,14 Now we need to enter into the secrets of the Lord's power being released through us as we pray in his name. This requires more than a mere repeating the formula "in Jesus' name" as we end a prayer. Are you making progress here?

14:16 **How many persons of the Trinity do you find in this verse?** The same is true with verse 26, as well as 15:26. **Do you think of the Holy Spirit as a very real person?** Write down your thinking, then turn to the *Special Helps* section, and read No. 1.

---

30. *Without breaking for the versification, read verse 12 again along with the next half dozen verses. Our greater works, then, are made possible by His going to the right hand of the Father. Christians everywhere can now pray in Jesus' name and thus see mighty things accomplished. Furhtermore, Jesus sends from glory the promised Holy Spirit to empower us for these accomplishments. 14:2 indicates that Jesus is also preparing our home of eternal enjoyment. All these are the present ministries of Christ.*

How can you show from this verse that the Holy Spirit *14:26*
is a real person?[31]

Let us suppose you are a Sunday School teacher and this *14:9*
is your text. From it you intend to prove that Jesus is truly
God the Son. You finish your lesson by quoting 5:18 and
10:30, adding, "Therefore, class, Jesus is equal with the
Father and is truly God." But one of your pupils interrupts
and with a deeply troubled look points to 14:28 where Jesus
says, "for the Father is greater than I." **Write down the
answer you would now give to your class.**[32]

Do not hesitate to read and pray aloud, using this verse. *14:27*
In place of the word "troubled," it might be helpful to insert
"anxious or agitated." And, in place of "afraid" use "craven
or cowardly."

Jesus gives a hint here of how our enemy operates. Various *14:30*
translations differ widely on the wording of the last clause
of the verse. Jesus realizes that Satan is returning for the
attack against Him and the Lord says (according to the
original Greek), "in me he has nothing" That is, try as he
will, the devil was to find no footing in Jesus' life. Our
Lord would offer no ground upon which Satan could stand
or even gain a toehold.

---

31. *Personal pronoun "He" refers to the Spirit. His work is to
teach, and that requires more than a vague influence. The Spirit
gives us personal instruction and counsel.*

32. *As a man, Jesus was submissive to His parents, paid taxes,
prayed to His Father, obeyed the law, washed His disciples' feet,
and could truly say that the Father was greater. However, when
He spoke as God (and He is that!) He could say in truth, "I and
my Father are one" (John 10:30). The manhood of Jesus was
used to image God's glory visibly before us. Praise God in prayer
as you read John 1:18; 2 Corinthians 4:6; Hebrews 1:1-3.*

Along the same line, Satan approaches us. He wants some compromise or unguarded area in our life. The devil makes a playground on every vacant lot. His aim is much more serious than pulling us into this or that temptation. He wants to gain an advantage over us, as 2 Corinthians 2:11 might be understood and translated.

Often we hear it asked, "Can a Christian be demon possessed?" If by possession one means an exchange in ownership, that could never be. However, we as God's children have a certain responsibility that goes with our freedom. Satan is, of course, going about in roaring anger, moving against any unguarded area. The question needs to be asked, what if we do not stand as men and wrestle against the enemy? What we give up, Satan can take over. Once he has leverage in a life, he will make it more difficult for that person to resist various sins. Simply making so many confessions to cover for so many sins is not God's way. In certain cases of repeated, habitual defeat, forgiveness alone is not enough. Deliverance is needed.

Rather than bogging ourselves down arguing over the meaning of "demon possession", let me put it this way: It is entirely possible for Christians to surrender an area of their life to our enemy — to fail in exercising their will and free-agency against him. With what terms shall we describe that sad, spiritual condition which now follows? It is not sufficient to say merely that a portion of the life is affected. A more helpful way of putting it might be to say that the subjected area is infected or perhaps infested.

It appears to me that habitual, repeated sin is virtually a choice to give up our right of choice. This exposes us to the devil in a peculiar way. Abandoning the control center of volition is serious business. Satan never passes an open door. Ephesians 4:26 is a familiar verse regarding anger. It should be read in conjunction with verse 27. It is shown that intense or protracted anger gives place to the devil. Angry, bitter people are, therefore, always deeply troubled people. In many cases I have encountered, simple confession of such an ingrained pattern is not enough. There must be a reclaiming of lost ground and an enlightened refusal to be subjected to Satan's domination any further in that particular area. Truly the blood of Jesus and His name has power enough to command deliverance for His obedient child.

Naturally, there are other causes for Satan's control over a life, such as occultism, a serious condition of hatred, passivity, deception, or a refusal to make restitution.

If needed, review comments on John 10:1-18 and 12:31.

What is meant by "fruit" in this chapter? [33]   *15:*

It is significant that the Son does not present Himself here *15:1* as the associate vinedresser with His Father. Rather, He places Himself in the soil, joined to us as a vine is joined to its branches. With this in mind, we are prepared for a profitable discussion of our life in Christ.

Picture the heavenly vinedresser approaching His plant *15:2* with knife drawn. What happens to those branches that are without fruit? What does He do to those that are bringing forth fruit? Both receive the knife and sometimes it may be as though we are being cut off when really we are being cut back.

---

33. Any gain on God's investment, whether in our own character or through us in the lives of others around. Examples: (1) Fruit of the Spirit (Galatians 5:22,23). (2) Good deeds (Colossians 1:10; Ephesians 2:10). (3) Reproduction through our witness. (4) Praise and worship (Hebrews 13:15).

Now think for a moment before writing. **What insrument of pruning does God much prefer to use?** [34]

The knife of Providence, then, is not God's generally preferred instrument. Of course, He does use life's pressures and sufferings, but much of that would be unnecessary if we submitted ourselves daily and prayerfully to pruning by the sword of the Spirit which is the Word of God. The clutter of agitated thinking, unclean imagination, carnal attitudes, and the like, would be cleansed and clipped from our lives to a great degree if we regularly submitted to the Scriptures in prayerful study. **Where are you now reading daily?** (See 2 Timothy 3:16-17.)

15:4-8 Discover the importance and deeper meaning of abiding in Christ. Apparently this is a conscious, continuing, living relationship.

Now, look into the connection between the Word of God and our abiding in Christ, verse 7.

What are the conditions for this broad promise of answered prayer (verse 7)? Are you meeting these conditions?

Now, notice the marked relationship between fruit and prayer by reading verse 7 and 8. See the same connection established also in verse 16 and 14:12-14.

15:9,15 How many are the privileges of being His! Pause and give thanks for truths expressed in the verses.

---

34. You will see it readily enough by reading the latter half of verse 2 along with verse 3. The words "prune" and "clean" are from the same root word. It is simply a garden term for clipping and clearing a plant of its undesirable growth. In a positive sense, pruning stimulates good growth and fruit.

If you are experiencing tension and opposition because *15:18-24* of your righteous life, beware of the film of discouragement tarnishing your outlook. If needed, study again the comments on John 7:7 and 10:19. See, also, Matthew 5:10-12, 44.

Compare verses John 15:22-25 with 9:39-41. Add to this 8:44 and surrounding verses. You will see readily enough why evil men plague good men.

Again we see all three Persons of the Trinity mentioned, *15:26-27* as in John 14:16 and 26.

You do not stand alone when you stand to witness for Christ. The Spirit aids you. Refer to Acts 5:32.

Assignment

1. Develop two lists as you go through this week:
   (1) Areas where you are claiming new deliverance from sin and Satan's hold — whether in attitudes, exercise of the will, control of the mind or emotions, imagination and other faculties.
   (2) Traits you are seeking to develop through Christ's life in you.
2. Prepare for next week's session by **reading John 16 and 17.**
3. **Memory verses: John 16:24; 1 Peter 5:7.**

Lesson IX
John 16 and 17

Things could not be worse. Killing for the glory of God! *16:1-4*
Jesus thus reminds us that it is impossible to expect men of
the world to appreciate and support us. Conflicts and
opposition are bound to develop, only let us not deserve it
(1 Peter 2:19, 20).

Looking especially at verse 7, how is it that the disciples, *16:7-16*
or we, are advantaged by having Jesus Christ absent
from us? Look very carefully into this question, because
many today seem to feel we are in an inferior age or stage
where not much happens in comparison with the life Jesus
and His disciples had together on earth. Keep the perspective
of God's progress with us throughout history. Perhaps you
find yourself forgetting the great provisions we now enjoy
and longing for the miracles of Bible days. Those wonder
works were scattered rather thinly over many centuries.
Read these words thoughtfully: "These were all commended
for their faith, yet none of them received what had been
promised. God had planned something better for us so that
only together with us would they be made perfect" (Heb.
11:39-40).

Beginning at verse 8 you are introduced to the ministry
of the Holy Spirit. Read with gratitude and recall our discussion on John 7:37-39 and 14:12-26.

**Write a list of various ministries of the Holy Spirit —
as many as you can recall.** [35]

16:26 Much vagueness clouds believers' minds concerning the
intercession of Christ. Here is a verse which will force us
to a clearer, more mature view of this present ministry of
our Savior. **What does Jesus mean when He says He will
not pray for us now?** [36]

16:33 Notice the two spheres in which we exist. Set this down
in your notebook. **What is to be our condition in each?**
What brings us the blessing of the spiritual sphere? What
encouragement is offered concerning the testing in the other
realm?

---

35. *A number of these ministries are shown to us in the Gospel
of John: convincing of sin, righteousness, and judgment (16:8-
11); regenerating (3:5-8); comforting (14:16-18); manifesting
Jesus (14:21; 16:10, 14-16); teaching (14:26; 16:12-15; see
1 John 2:20, 27, also); empowering to witness (15:26-27; Acts
1:8, 5:32). Of course, there are many other functions of the Spirit,
such as making us like Jesus in character (Galatians 5:22-23);
assisting us in putting to death evil desires and doings (Romans
8:13); and helping us pray (Romans 8:26-27). Is this fullness
yours? Pray over these insights, thanking God for each one as
you search the Scriptures.*

36. *Study verse 27. Always seek the answer by reading the
context — verses before and after the verse in question. Jesus is
saying that He will not have to beg the Father on our behalf. His
intercession is not a vocal begging. His Person is Divine and He
is beloved of the Father. His work has entirely satisfied the
Father. And, His position is one of honor and victory. The Father
is now more than willing to bless us who believe because we are
rightly related to the Son.*

What special doctrine about the Son of God is implied *17:5, 24*
in each of these verses? [37]

What other teachings about Jesus Christ do you learn *17:8, 20*
from these verses? Also, add verses 2-4.

The torch of truth is passed from the Father in heaven down to man and onward in history. **Can you trace the route of this movement?** [38]

Notice the first link in the chain of events mentioned above has been successful. Jesus says, "I have brought you glory on earth by completing the work you gave me to do" (verse 4). It appears now that His chief concern is to keep the torch alive and glowing as it is received by His humble band of disciples. His prayer continues, " I will remain in the world no longer, but they are still in the world, and I am coming to you. Holy Father, protect them by the power of your name — the name you gave me . . . . My prayer is not that you take them out of the world but that you protect them from the evil one" (verses 11, 15).

Prayer is the mighty means Jesus employs to protect His followers and see His plan carried to success. According to verse 9 His prayer is pointed and selective. "I pray for them," that is, His very own followers. Then He adds the chilling, awesome words, " I am not praying for the world," (verse 9).

---

37. *His pre-existance. That is, Jesus of Nazareth is the eternal Son of God, existing forever. Before the world was He always was and ever will be. That is why He accepted worship in His human form while on earth. See implications of John 8:58.*

38. *The Son receives the words given by the Father. These are received and believed by the disciples. Finally, subsequent generations of believers are in view in verse 20 as they believe through the early disciples' efforts. Still further, the world is affected as we later believers live as we should (verse 21).*

How great is the ignorance and folly of sinful men who sport their way through life, vainly imagining they are under the prayerful protection of a Savior!

Much help can be obtained from this chapter in determining the nature of our future glories. In light of all this, what should be our present priorities?

17:11 Kept.

17:13-16 Joy despite opposition. See 15:11; 16:24, 33; 1 Thessalonians 5:16; 1 Peter 1:8. Remember Romans 8:28. **Being so concerned that His faithful ones not fall into evil (verse 15), why did not Jesus take them with Him out of the world?** See verse 20. Now check Romans 10:9-15.

17:18 We are sent to obey as Jesus did (cf. verse 4).

Assignment

1. Practice remembering the Person and presence of the Holy Spirit. In the light of 16:14, set your mind much on Jesus this week (Colossians 3:1, 2; Psalm 16:8).

2. **Read John 18 and 19** in preparation for next week's session.

3. Look up the word **vicar** and **vicarious** in the dictionary and write your findings for next week's discussion.

4. **Memorize Romans 8:28,** making sure that you avoid popular misquotations of this verse.

Lesson X
John 18 and 19

18:1, 2   Demons sometimes roam Gethsemane's ground. Judas knew Jesus' favorite place of prayer. Now under the devil's control (John 13:27), he did not hesitate to lead the enemy band to the sacred territory. Always remember that the devil knows your place of prayer. **What are common difficulties you face, along with other believers, as you kneel to pray? List them.** [39]

The disciples' failure to resist the onslaught of pressure is significant. Jesus sought to stir them to prayer. They gave up and sank repeatedly into the false escape of sleep. See the parallel accounts in Matthew 26, Mark 14, and Luke 22.

18:5, 18   See where both Judas and Peter stand, noting the identical words in each case: "standing with them." **Think back over the collapse and failure in each life and list as many parallels as you can.** [40]

Beware of stumbling over others. For a time, the counterfeit (Judas) might look like the fallen believer (Peter). However, they are very different, as the end shows. Judas horribly destroyed himself, whereas Peter preached in the same locality and thousands repented. Sometimes it requires patience and discernment to distinguish between those who

---

39. *Wandering thoughts, tiredness, a distracting busyness, lustful imagination, guilt feelings or a sense of unworthiness.*

40. *Judas betrayed Jesus; Peter said, "I don't know this man" and used cursing to underscore and enforce his denial (Luke 22:71). In grief, Judas returned the silver with which he was bribed; Peter wept bitterly upon realizing what he had done. Here the parallel ends.*

have turned from the fold. Some will end in destruction.
Others, in restoration. Even their sorrow was of an essentially
different quality, as 2 Corithians 7:10 explains:

> Godly sorrow brings repentance that leads to salvation
> and leaves no regret, but worldly sorrow brings death.

Tares (weeds) that did not look like wheat would serve no
purpose for the enemy who sows them. Sometimes the tares
appear to outshine the wheat. Don't be stumbled.

Humiliation. The prelude to crucifixion. **Make a list of
all the indignities suffered by our Lord in these two
chapters.** *18: 19:*

**When we say Jesus suffered *vicariously*, what does that
mean?** Review the meanings of "vicar" and "vicarious"
you found in the dictionary assignment.

An alternate term for vicar is substitute. To say Jesus
died vicariously is to say He died a substitionary death.

Two large meanings are impregnated in the statement,
Christ lived and died for us. "For us" might mean His
assistance to us as an example. More importantly, however,
it implies He was a substitute for us. Both His life and His
death can be viewed from these two points of view.

Consider His life. It was lived for us as an example. More
than that, His perfectly righteous life was lived on our
behalf, in order that we might have His record credited to
our account.

Now consider His death. It was an example of holy heroism
and peaceful acquiescense to the Father's will. However,
the largest emphasis in Scripture is on the substitutionary
aspect of His death. Christ died in our place, in our stead,
paying our legal debt. Once released from all charges
against us, we are not simply returned to ground level zero.
But the holy life (the positive righteousness) of Jesus Christ,

wherein He perfectly obeyed every law and commandment of His Father, is credited to our account.

While reading this section of John's gospel, have the scenes of Jesus' suffering and death passed before your eyes? You are witnessing the fulfillment of John 1:29. Read aloud Leviticus 17:11 and give thanks to God in prayer.

Heb. 9:8 Examine carefully each occurance of the word "con-
9, 13, 14. science." **What is the difference between the Old Testament**
10:1, 2, **sacrifices and the sacrifice of Jesus Christ, as to the**
22 **effect of each on man's troubled conscience?** [41]

What is the connection between the new covenant and man's new relief of conscience? Exactly how does this come about? Let me put it this way: **Explain the effective "mechanics" of it**. [42]

The conscience then is relieved when we view the sacrifice as God views it and value it as God values it. And, He says, "Their sins and lawless acts I will remember no more." Further, "And where these have been forgiven, there is no longer any sacrifice for sin" (verses 17, 18). Rely on this and your conscience will be released.

---

41. The old covenant brought no relief. The new covenant is intended to bring full release.

42. A prayerful perusal of the first half of Hebrews 10 will bring you into the heart of this encouraging truth. The cessation of the sacrifice indicates its perfection in God's eyes. All is fulfilled. The will of God is satisfied and the Priest may now be seated, ceasing His struggle against sin (Hebrews 10:1-12). In the Old Testament period, the repeated scarifices left the worshipers with imperfect, troubled consciences (verses 1-3), but now "by one sacrifice he has made perfect forever those who are being made holy" (verse 14).

At the Lord's table, we are most certainly not repeating a sacrifice. Clearly, we are remembering what Jesus did. We participate "in remembering" His suffering and death vicariously. The one perfect offering on Calvary, therefore, means the ceasing of the sacrifice and assures us that our consciences may be relieved from all guilt clouds.

With these teachings fixed in your mind, tackle this question: **What is the real evil in allowing our consciences to continue being disturbed with feelings of accusation and guiltiness?** [43]

The quality of the sacrifice should determine the condition of the conscience.

---

43. *It would be a testimony against the perfection of Christ's sacrifice on the cross. In the light of Hebrews 10, an unrelieved conscience implies that one is relying upon an imperfect sacrifice, which, no matter how often repeated or called to mind does not seem to satisfy the Father in heaven. So, our sins would then remain in remembrance against us. Praise God, the converse is actually true in Jesus Christ!*

Assignment

1. List problems you encounter this week as you pray and note also what you do about them.

2. List helpful Scriptures you employ this week for the cleansing and relief of your conscience.

3. Prepare for the next lesson by **reading John 20 and Colossians 3.**

4. **Memory Verse: Romans 5:8.**

Lesson XI
John 20, Colossians 3:1-5

Let us dedicate these next moments together for capturing the reality and significance of the resurrection of the Lord Jesus Christ. *20:1-18*

First, read the John text. Place yourself in the garden scene. Allow no lurking doubts regarding the factual history here. Jesus rose bodily from cold, real death just as He predicted. Read the accounts and choose to believe them.

List the following Scripture references down the left-hand edge of your notebook: Romans 5:10; 1 Corinthians 15:1-23; Hebrews 7:25; 1 John 2:1, 2; Acts 2:32, 33. **Look up each verse and comment briefly on the benefits now yours through the resurrection of the Lord.** This will be extended still further in our final two sessions.

Notice John the author moves from the confession of Thomas to a statement of his own purpose in writing the Gospel. **What is that purpose, according to verse 31?** *20:24-31* Are you certain this has been achieved in your life as you have pursued these studies? Please kneel right now in prayer and acknowledge deliberately and clearly that Jesus is the Christ, the chosen Savior, and the Son of God. State definitely that you, with Thomas, bow to Him as Lord, that is, Divine Master, the One who has absolute right over you. Name and yield any areas of conflict.

We shall here take a two-week break from Scripture in John, returning finally for Chapter 21. Now give your attention to a most important area of truth in which we shall invest our concluding studies together.

An almost universal cry from the hearts of earnest Christians is: How can I stop sinning repeatedly and live a holy life pleasing to God? Many feel as if they are explosive bundles walking about through temptation's flames. Repeatedly they are kindled in a new outburst of evil passion.

For them, the number one mystery is how to reconcile Scripture's description of the Christian life with what is experienced. You are dead to sin, says the Word, but perhaps you are all too conscious of pounding evil desires and proneness toward sin. Certain sins may seem a characteristic tendency in your life. How can one be dead and yet so very much alive, stimulated and stirred by temptation? The answer is not as complicated as some make it. Simply, we are dead in one way, but in another quite alive.

For a moment let's back away and get an overview of things. You and I have two large problems as we first come to Christ. (1) We are legally guilty before God. (2) We are prone toward sin. As our Savior, Jesus releases us from this double bondage in a twofold manner. First, He stands in our place before the bar of justice and pays our great sin debt by dying on the cross. Once this payment cancels our guilt, our record before God is completely altered. Guilt is gone and the perfect righteousness of Christ is added to our account. Second, our Lord works to release us in our actual experience from the power of sin working within us. This is accomplished by granting us deeper insights into the provisions of grace and by giving us adequate means to appropriate it all. I will now guide you into a Bible examination of these powerful truths. [44]

---

44. *Much of the following material over the next several pages is taken from my book,* People Helping People. *See the chapter headed, "Lesson Two: Our Indentification with Christ."*

Here is a simple procedure which has proven helpful to me. Write on a slip of paper the words "obligations" and "provisions." **Ask yourself which of these terms is the more basic in God's plan of grace? Do we fulfill certain obligations and thus gain God's provisions? Or, is it the other way around — we accept His provisions and thus are enabled to fulfill the obligations? [45]**

Take another sheet of paper and strike a line down the middle. At the heading of the left-hand side write "provisions." The word "obligations" then goes over the other column. Turn to Colossians 3 and proceed with the following progression of questions and statements. *Col. 3:3-5*

At verse 3 underscore the words "you died" and "with Christ."

> For *you died,* and your life is now hidden *with Christ* in God. (Col. 3:3)

Now dropping down to verse 5, underscore the words "put to death."

> *Put to death,* therefore, whatever belongs to your earthly nature: sexual immorality, impurity, lust, evil desires and greed, which is idolatry. (Col. 3:5)

In order, answer these questions: **According to verse 3, what died? When did this death occur? How do you explain the seeming contradiction between verse 3 and verse 5?** (First we are told that we Christians are dead

---

45. *Obviously, the order of grace is: God's provisions are laid down first and only by standing on that basis do we gain strength to obey and fulfill obligations. Bear in mind that the term provisions refers to all Christ freely gives — His life and death for us and the help to live a new life. Obligations refers to God's commands and to our responsibilities as His children.*

indeed, and next we are told that we have yet to experience a putting to death and are to get on with it.) [46]

Which of these verses (3 or 5) is stated as a provision? (That is, in which are we simply informed of what Jesus Christ has done for us?) **And, which is stated as a command or obligation?** Place key phrases of each verse in the appropriate column of your paper.

What is the significance of the word "therefore" in verse 5? It harkens back to verse 3, establishing the order of the whole teaching. "For you died . . . with Christ," *therefore* "put to death." Provisions are laid down as the basis and we are "therefore" instructed to fulfill the obligations of calling a halt to the rule of sin over us. Gracious provisions are to find expression in the life.

---

46. What died? According to Colossians 3:3, I died. This answer cannot be improved on. Let it stand just as the Word here says it. We are not told that my sin nature died, my sins died, or any part of me died. It is simply stated that I died in my representative Jesus Christ.

When did this death occur? If I died with Him, then this occurred when He died. That was 2,000 years ago. True, it becomes real to me when I am born anew and begin to understand, but God counts it that I died when Jesus died.

The next real test comes when you attempt to put into words how it is that the believer is dead (verse 3), and yet he still faces the obligation to put sin to death (verse 5). This is not, of course, a contradiction because there is one sense in which we have already died and there is another sense in which we are still too much alive.

We are in Christ dead (executed for sin) but in our actual experience we are yet alive to the allurements of sin and thus are called on to put evil tendencies and appetites to death.

Another verse which might be studied with great profit is 2 Corinthians 5:14.

> For Christ's love compels us,
> because we are convinced
> that one died for all, and therefore all died.

Note carefully the way I have divided the verse into three meaningful parts. Here the apostle tells us the secret of a life motivated by Christ's love. Can you say with Paul, "Christ's love compels" me? You will be able to say this when you reach the conviction to which he came. Read the remainder of the verse again. It seems to require special illumination of the Spirit to see the depth of that statement: "If one died for all, then all died" (Amplified).

Write the two halves of this special proposition, one beneath the other.

> If one died for all,
> then all died.

Underscore the words "if" and "then." This indicates that if the first statement is true then the second follows. Next, circle the words "one" and "all." If One was the stand-in for all, then all died when He died. That is, we believers died by proxy in Jesus Christ. If He is our duly appointed representative, then God counts us as having been executed for our sins. That is precisely what happened at Calvary.

It might be true that I have not yet put to death sin in my experience as I ought. But it is nevertheless quite true that I died via my substitute Jesus Christ.

These Scriptures might be lined up on the Provision and Obligation Chart you began earlier as we indicate in the following diagram.

Provision		Obligation
(to be received, believed, claimed)		(to be obeyed)
"For you died, . . . with Christ" Col. 3:3	*therefore*	"Put to death," Col. 3:5
"If ONE died for ALL then ALL DIED." 2 Cor. 5:14 (Amplified)		
"For we know that our old self was crucified with him		that we should no longer be slaves to sin" Rom. 6:6

We have seen thus far that Christ died not only to free us from sin's penalty but also to break sin's absolute power over us. Turn to the most important of all Scriptural selections on this theme — Romans 6. Here is set forth the true basis for victory over sin, namely, our identity with Christ. God accepts Him on our behalf. We are counted in Him.

See Romans 6:6. Even though we are descendants of Adam, God considers that connection as officially ended. In that regard, we were executed via our Substitute 2,000 years ago. Presently, we shall see more exactly what our "old man" is.

Allow me to review — going over the same ground once more. Prayerfully attempt to grasp it more clearly.

How do you explain the apparent contradiction between Colossians 3:3 and verse 5? The third verse says we are already officially dead, having been put to death in our Substitute. The fifth verse shows, however, that we are by no means insensible to temptation and we are responsible to see that a dying to various lusts takes place.

Notice the former is announced as a *provision*. Since Jesus was our Substitute, God counts Calvary's crucifixion as having happened to us. Then verse 5 is a command, but the *obligation* is based upon the *provision*. Note the word "therefore."

Always bear in mind that God deals with us according to grace, not law. Thus, in the chart His provisions enable us to fulfill our obligations. God first informs us, "I have done thus and so for you." Then follows the command, "You can and must therefore do thus and so." Even with regard to the obligations, He graciously works within us, as we shall presently show.

Assignment

1. Meditate much over truths taught in this lesson and explain them to one or two Christian friends.

2. **Read Romans 6, 7, 8** and draw up a list of five or six key phrases or statements of the main teachings in Chapter 6. Make a couple of basic statements to summarize what you see in Chapter 7. Sketch the movement of truths in 8:1-13 using several key statements.

3. **Memory Verse: Hebrews 7:25.**

Lesson XII
Romans 6, 7, 8

Confusing, fuzzy words said confidently are no adequate explanation of God's plan for releasing us from sin. We are not called to believe anything that is contrary to fact. In gaining victory over sin, God does not assign us the task of believing so intensely, contrary to appearance, that we finally experience it as so. Rather, our victory moves within grasp when we come to know more exactly in what sense the Scripture says we are dead to sin and alive to God, and in what sense sin is yet a "live issue."

Have in hand your written assignment for Romans 6, 7, 8.

The intention of grace is to enable us to keep from sin, not simply to guarantee forgiveness as we continue to sin. We are so instructed by the very truth symbolized in water baptism. Our baptism says that we are indeed united with Christ in His death, and also in His resurrection. This union is accomplished by God in Christ as a gracious gift. *Rom. 6:1-5* *cf. 2 Cor. 5:15*

Once informed and "knowing" of our identity and inclusion in Jesus' substitutionary death, we have next to discover what is meant when it speaks here of our "old self." **Write your explanation.**[47] *Rom. 6:6*

---

47. *What I was formerly in my relationship with Adam. Notice 1 Corinthians 15:45 calls Jesus "the last Adam." Jesus stood at the end of the old creation. When Adam sinned he ruined the entire order we call the First or Old Man. Our substitute Jesus Christ stood in place of the whole old order and in effect ended it at the cross.*

Rising from the dead, Jesus Christ heads the new creation. Whether we live before or after His earthly ministry, God counts believers as having died and risen with, and in, Christ. "My old (former) self (man)" is simply my lot and share in the old Adam lineup. For further discussion and diagrams, see Chapter 7 of my book, People Helping People.

87

Perhaps your answer tended to obscure the distinction between "our old self" and "the body of sin." If that was so, it would leave you with a fuzzy mass of indefinite teaching. You see, the Apostle is saying that I, as I once was (the old man), "was crucified with him so that the body of sin might be done away with, that we should no longer be slaves to sin." The movement of truth is clear. Our identity in Jesus' crucifixion is for the purpose of making the body of sin powerless (or another way of putting it: to break the grip of the flesh) and this is to lead to a new freedom in practice. Notice there are three parts to the verse. Draw three good sized blocks in a row across your paper. **In each block write the key expression of each part of the verse, noting by connecting arrows that the first leads to the second and the second leads to the third. [48]**

What we were without Christ (in Adam) is now declared ended and what we are in Christ is begun! This crucifixion, in the first part of Romans 6:6, is related to Colossians 3:3.

Rom. 6:7   This little verse which immediately follows is so often misunderstood! This verse does *not* mean we are unresponsive or insensitive to sin. It is merely saying that since God truly counts us as having been executed through our Substitute Jesus, no legal charges stand against us, whatsoever. We are thereby acquitted. See the marginal reading of the NAS on this verse.

Rom. 6:8-11   Our twofold union with Christ — in death and in new life. Our death via the cross has reference to sin and all its punishment. Our life, springing from the resurrection of our Lord, is "to God."

Again, this section is not teaching that we are dead to sin in the sense of being unresponsive to it. That simply is not

48.
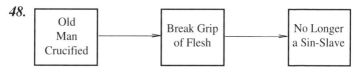

true. Jesus is said to have "died to sin once for all" (verse 10). That is exactly our condition. We died through our Substitute. In the official execution for sin, which is death, now we are free from condemnation. Becoming unresponsive to sin and freed from its ongoing strength within is quite another matter, which we will take up shortly.

Reading verses 10 and 11 together shows that we are to consider ourselves as having "died to sin" when Christ "died to sin." But what does this mean? Surely, He did not have to put down inner sin! He was answering to the charges against us.

The sin spoken of here is the legal guilt and condemnation charged to all mankind by God. Review how the term "sin" is used in Scripture, "Special Helps," No. 2. Now you should see that the "death to sin" spoken of in verses 2, 7, 10 and 11 refers to the payment of sin's penalty, which is death. In other words, Christ's death answers to the charges of our guilt. And as Colossians 3:3 says, "... you died with Christ."

Thus, these verses are not speaking of our "deadness" to the powerful pull of sin. Rather, they inform us of a most gracious provision which must not be trifled with. Let me expand on verse 2 to read like this: "With reference to the guilt (sin) that once condemned us, we were executed (died) via our Substitute. How then could we ever turn back into that which cost so much!" See how this view agrees with 7,10 and 11. Make Christ's death your death. Not until you have settled sin's debt can you move on to Colossians 3:5 and put to death sin in your day by day experience.

A Christian going along in sin is unthinkable. What Jesus Christ accomplished on our behalf He now desires to work out in us. We must, therefore, claim in our day by day experience what belongs to us in Jesus Christ. *Rom. 6:12-14*

89

Here is God's call to quit the life of sin. We are not to allow ourselves to be bent by the lust and cravings of evil desire. God wants all our faculties.

Seek to see the distinction between what Christ did in your place, on your behalf, in your stead as your Substitute, and, on the other hand, what He waits to do in you in this present day.

Bring out verse 14 for special study. **Does any sin tend to control your will?** Perhaps you are painfully aware of a tendency to fail repeatedly, yet you seem unable to escape. If that is true, pay particular attention to this question: **What reason is given here in verse 14 for there being no necessity for continuing to sin?** [49]

Scripture presents a twofold view of grace: (1) Christ in my place, (2) Christ in me. In the first, Christ pays my sin debt. In the second, He enables me to put down sin and live righteously. Christ in my behalf on the one hand, and Christ within me on the other. This is the complete divine arrangement of grace. Whether or not this scheme seems to be working effectively in your case or mine, it is nonetheless entirely sufficient if understood and embraced.

Rom. 7   Check your written statements on this chapter. God's law is here shown to be good, but it exposes our inability to live right and leaves us a frustrated victim of our own evil tendencies. Rescue from our sinful nature can come only through Jesus Christ.

---

49. *Because we are under an arrangement of grace rather than of law.*

90

What a position we are in! When Satan comes to tempt us, he whispers "grace." After we have fallen into sin, he shouts "the Law!" [50]

Again, Jesus' twofold help. On our behalf He settles the threatened legal judgment against us. Next, He helps us live according to God's good will. Once sin is legally settled and guilt is gone, I am no longer under authority of sin. It is no longer necessary that I be in sin's bondage. I am now free to have God's gracious help. *Rom. 8:1-4*

The question arises: **In light of all these teachings, why then does one still experience serious failures — often repeatedly?** [51]

Look first at verse 13 and discover the means or the instrument God uses for helping us put to death the outgrowth of the sin nature. [52] *Rom. 8:5-14*

What is taught here in Scripture bears upon our provision/obligation chart. Check it again and bear in mind that the Holy Spirit now becomes our helper enabling us to fulfill the obligations. We are not left simply to some deeper life

---

50. *First, the tempter would have us take wrongful advantage of grace. He would have us look upon grace as a plan to make it possible to safely continue in sin. But grace enables us to quit sin. Understood correctly, it never invites lax living. After one has fallen into sin, of course, the accuser will change his tune and talk forcefully about the Law and the condemnation it threatens.*

51. *There are two reasons. (1) The basic identity truths already taught are not understood, or else (2) The benefits of grace are being considered as automatic. That is not true, however. God requires us to use certain means of grace. More of that next session.*

52. *The Holy Spirit.*

formula of teaching which must be believed hard enough in order to put down the outbreak of sin. No, Christ vitally lives within through the operation of the Holy Spirit. The Spirit, then, produces His fruit in our character (Galatians 5:22, 23). **What fruit of the Spirit can you list before you look up these verses?** Notice particularly the ones not lodged in your memory. This Scripture will also show you that those walking in the Spirit always find themselves within the Law and not scraping the fences.

Assignment

1. Review repeatedly the truths taught in this study.
2. Make a special point in your praying that God will make it clear enough to you for your own relief and for the good of others.
3. **Study again Romans 8:1-14. Read John 21.**
4. **Memory Verse: 2 Corinthians 5:17.**

Lesson XIII
Romans 8, John 21

As we look further into the teachings of Romans 8, examine at the same time the statements you prepared two lessons ago on this section of Scripture.

Rom. 8:5 **What terms in this verse indicate the basic roots of the two types of men?** [53]

How does this root express itself in life? [54]

Rom. 8:6-8 **Is it possible for a professing Christian to avoid a showdown with a wrong mind-set or carnal outlook?** [55]

Rom. 8:9 Notice the uncompromising condition established in the life by the Spirit of God. Furthermore, this is said to be the case with each man who is a true Christian. The sinful involvements and compromise of carnality are contradictory therefore to the very essence of the Christian life.

Undoubtedly, we should now explain further how the Christian may have conquest over sin within his life and how it is that defeat is such a distinct possibility in spite of the large provisions of grace. Obviously, mere desire, intention or hopefulness is not enough. There must be the exercising of those means given by God, for the subduing of the flesh and the elevation of the Spirit. This will include the diligent exercise of prayer, regular reading of Scripture,

---

53. *"According to the sinful nature" and "in accordance with the Spirit" or in the NAS "according to the flesh" and "according to the Spirit."*

54. *With a frame of mind or outlook that is in keeping with the root. The verse, therefore, describes two vastly different ways of living and looking at life.*

55. *No.*

and faithful attendance at the meetings of God's family, the church. Where these means of spiritual vitality are exercised, God's Spirit will work more freely in the life, putting down evil desires (Romans 8:13).

Jesus once gave plain warning to his sleepy disciples, "Watch and pray so that you will not fall into temptation. The spirit is willing, but the body is weak" (Mark 14:38). Paul taught the Galatians about these same two opposing currents. "For the sinful nature desires what is contrary to the Spirit, and the Spirit what is contrary to the sinful nature. They are in conflict with each other, so that you do not do what you want" (Gal. 5:17).

Whenever the believer is delinquent in feeding on Scripture, breathing invigorating heavenly air through prayer and seeking encouragement and strength in the congregation of the Lord, his lower nature will prevail. It will never end in a mere draw.

There is no way to avoid the pain of crucifying the flesh; the only question is, how am I, in my weakness, to do it? The answer is not complicated.

First, there must be no "sowing to the flesh." I mean by that, not doing things which stimulate or indulge the desires of our sinful nature. In other words, do not feed and strengthen the wild tiger you must fight. "Rather, clothe yourselves with the Lord Jesus Christ, and do not think about how to gratify the desires of the sinful nature" (Rom. 13:14).

Second, renew a diligent exercise of the means of grace already mentioned. Prayerfully cooperate with the Spirit as lusts are put to death.

Now, let us return to Romans 8:9 and summarize. The Christian is fundamentally different from the unbeliever. The former has been regenerated by the Holy Spirit and has that same Spirit in his life, according to verse 9. He is fundamentally, basically not "of the flesh" ("controlled by the sinful nature"). However, both Scripture and experience teach us that carnality ever lurks within even the believer's heart. Once these tendencies are aroused and the passions indulged, the Spirit's control seems to recede and during this contradictory period it will appear that even the child of God is "according to the sinful nature."

It is no surprise that any man whose carnality is aroused will want the wrong. Many feeling the strength of evil desires become hopelessly discouraged and question their total relationship with Christ. If that should be your case, or if you know of one in such a condition, here are steps out of it:

1. Make a definite affirmation of personal faith in Jesus Christ as Lord and Savior. Do this in prayer.

2. Review and claim the truths of our identity with Christ in His death and resurrection.

3. Review and claim the power and ever present help of God's Spirit to enable us to live holy lives and to say no to sin (Romans 8:13).

4. Through prayer and Scripture reading, and memorizing Bible verses, your spirit can be quickened again and the flesh crucified.

5. Take the position that no known compromise or cheating with a pet sin is allowable. Such a situation feeds the flesh and grieves the Spirit. Defeat may always be expected in such a case.

The peculiar problems relating to habit-type sins will be discussed in Part 3, Chapter III, "Additional Teachings." Perhaps you will, in the course of sharing these studies with others, have opportunity to help loose these very wearisome chains from some.

Returning to John's Gospel, we witness the touching *21:15-17* restoration of an erring disciple by the Lord Himself. Peter now experiences the true "footwashing" he once had thought to refuse in its physical symbol (John 13:3-10).

Turning one back into the way of forgiveness and holiness is a very great work, according to James 5:19-20. **Write down one or two names of those who are wavering spiritually and who might be your responsibility.** Pray for them over the next several days and then, as God directs, offer them help by praying with them and sharing helpful truths. Prepare yourself for this by studying Galatians 6:1 and 2 Timothy 2:24-26.

Keep in mind the setting of our Lord's discussion with *21:18-22* Peter. He does not first call him to follow and serve. The affirmation of love precedes this. First is, "Do you truly love me?" Next is, "Follow me." In order, the third concern is what we shall do as our life ministry. Then what are our spiritual capacities and gifts to perform our particular ministries? One should not sit waiting for a mysterious "call" but should take practical steps to devote himself in loving service to Christ. Passivity should be avoided. Should only pastors and missionaries pray to find their slot in life service? Ought not all believers do this?

Allow the Spirit of God to spread before you the panorama of His varied endowments of spiritual equipment for preaching, teaching, exhorting, helping, performing acts of mercy, giving, evangelism, and the like. Study basic passages on this subject, such as Romans 12; 1 Corinthians 12, 13, 14; 1 Peter 4:7-11. Make notes on what you learn. Remember, the attitude with which a spiritual capacity is developed and used is of first importance. The fruit of the Spirit before the gifts of the Spirit. Also, be concerned with the best gifts first, as Scripture instructs us.

At all costs avoid the two types of pride warned of in 1 Corinthians 12 — (1) inferiority, verses 15-18 (2) superiority, verses 19-25. **Which of these appears to be more your tendency?**

If you are overburdened in Christian service of any kind, the problem might be one of several things. First, you might simply be weary in your well doing — in need of refreshment. Attend to this directly by counseling and praying with others and seeking new rest and renewal from God. It might be, too, that there is a reservation and unwillingness in your service. Any resistance on our part cuts down the power supply and makes everything drag. Or, it might be that you have been misguided in your efforts and are attempting to minister where you have not the spiritual capacities to do so. Once you ascertain that to be the case, you ought to cease (gracefully and without regret) struggling to do what God has not called and equipped you to do. Feel no guilt in making this adjustment. Be open to counsel from others, but in the end you must obey God rather than man.

Here are some practical steps to take if you are uncertain of your personal gifts from God for service:

1. Meditate on Scripture and have definite prayer.
2. Gain experience serving. Invest effort. Observe results.
3. Seek confirmation by the church. Perhaps ask counsel and a time of consecration with the church leaders. Make very certain that you have the high view of the local church as given in the New Testament. All Christ's people make up the church. The Church exists on earth as local assemblies. That is our Lord's great expression of Himself in the world today. Your church, with its weaknesses and needs — if it is at all true to God's Word — is the Body of Christ!

Hopefully, you will be led to share these Spiritual Life Studies with others. It is a life-changing work! When Jesus returns, may He find you happily engaged in His service, shoulder to shoulder with brothers and sisters you love and who love you.

> But you, dear friends, build yourselves up in your most holy faith and pray in the Holy Spirit. Keep yourselves in God's love as you wait for the mercy of our Lord Jesus Christ to bring you to eternal life. Be merciful to those who doubt; snatch others from the fire and save them; to others show mercy, mixed with fear — hating even the clothing stained by corrupted flesh.

> To him who is able to keep you from falling and to present you before his glorious presence without fault and with great joy — to the only God our Savior be glory, majesty, power and authority, through Jesus Christ our Lord, before all ages, now and forevermore! Amen. (Jude 20-25)

Part 3

The Leader's Preparation

I

Objectives: Know What You
Are Trying to Accomplish

An Important Word of Explanation: It needs to be crystal clear that we are shifting gears at this point, and I shall now address all that follows to those who have completed the Spiritual Life Studies and have an interest in reviewing and sharing them with others. (Blessed indeed are those who have someone to lead them personally through the sessions.)

According to Ephesians 4:11, 12 all believers are expected to have some vital function in the Lord's service. Leaders of the church are to see to that. One day, all of us will give an account of our ministries. We must not allow one another to slumber on in ineffectiveness.

If God so directs you, after you have completed the SLS, dedicate your life to lead others through these studies. Soon you will see numbers of your friends begin living more meaningful lives and some serving with you as SLS leaders. Remember, it will be far more beneficial to them if they are guided through these sessions by you personally, rather than receiving the Manual first.

Make it your aim to get your partner out in the trenches, into areas of productivity in the church and more vital functioning as husband, wife, parent, son or daughter. To do this you will need to know the ABC steps or lessons in edification. Perhaps you often have used in your witnessing the ABC steps of evangelism. But now, let us consider the pattern which God's Spirit seems to use in developing so many of His children. Then we shall relate that to these Spiritual Life Studies. The next several pages are taken from Chapter 5 in my book *People Helping People*, published by the author. (Several succeeding chapters in

103

that book demonstrate in more depth the use of lessons in edification)

These lessons really indicate levels of spiritual growth. They also may be thought of as a prescribed route over which you might take a son or daughter or a Christian friend whom you would assist spiritually. Finally, this list may serve as an index for discovering where one is bogged down. By it you soon can determine what lesson is due next or what particular teaching he or she may have missed.

Here are the lessons for individual edification:
1. A more serious view of sin.
2. A new view of our identification with Christ.
3. The filling of the Holy Spirit.
4. My place and ministry in the local church.
5. The spiritual warfare.
6. Life of intercession.

Now you will deduce that if a person has not reached level number one, but is one of those half-hearted, coasting Christians, there will be a hardened type of indifference. Of course, many such persons are very dutiful and active in religious works. These will not be, however, a true responsiveness to the Lord and His fellowship.

Let's go a step further. Suppose one has been brought into this first level of experience through a new working of the Holy Spirit but does not yet experience and see the second truth listed above, what will he be like? Will he not be discouraged and depressed?

The second growth lesson involves understanding how Christ not only died for me but I died with Him and rose with Him. Can you explain the seeming contradiction between Colossians 3:3 and verse 5? How did we die with Christ? In what sense are we still having to put to death? When did verse 3 take place? How does verse 5 take place? Of course, Romans 6, 7, 8 is the basic passage here, along with other texts as 2 Corinthians 5:14-21 and Galatians 5.

Suppose, however, a believer even with these truths in his heart finds the spiritual life beginning to be a dry, hard pull for him. Chances are he needs to know that our union with Christ is meant to bring us the benefits of the Holy Spirit's fullness in our lives. Acts 2:32, 33 needs to be studied and even diagrammed. (See our discussion under John 7:37-39.) Note the route the Holy Spirit takes to reach us. Now our Representative is in glory to share this supreme gift with us. Truly Jesus' great ministry in mediation not only rids us of sin but provides us with the blessed Spirit (Galatians 3:14). The body has full rights to all that our exalted Head receives on our behalf.

Believers, who make up Christ's Body, are all baptized in the Spirit (1 Corinthians 12:13), but the filling is not automatic and therefore we are commanded to avail ourselves of it, exercising our will and choice (Ephesians 5:18). The filling of the Spirit is normal, but I say again, it is not automatic.

Next, if you discover one who is quite a "deeper life buff" and yet is either somewhat frustrated or a bit too independent in attitude and stance, I would then question whether such a one is a vital part of a real assembly of believers. Perhaps he has not moved on to this step in his spiritual pilgrimage.

Christians need to know what their life-ministry is to be. Scripture teaches each believer is to exercise the particular Spirit equipment God has given. This is more than natural talent (Romans 12; 1 Corinthians 12-14; Ephesians 4; 1 Peter 4:10, 11).

Now, it is possible to have achieved all the forgoing levels of insights and development and still be erratic, compulsive, and perhaps depressed. Some apparently mature and experienced Christians are very flammable and difficult to predict. At times they seem driven. It could be that they have yielded certain areas to Satan's control. Perhaps they have little knowledge of how to resist and war

105

against the enemy. This is disastrous. Satan has many more designs against us than getting us to "come on and do this bad thing." Study John 14:30; 2 Corinthians 2:11; Ephesians 4:27. From these texts, what is Satan really trying to gain?

Finally, all should develop a life of true intercessory prayer. The sooner the better. Probably, struggles in the earlier progress will spur one to deepen the prayer life. Happy the Christian with a friend who knows how to pray and how to put some of the secrets into words. Obviously, this has to be done with discretion. But how refreshing and helpful it is to have someone put their hand on your shoulder and point you into a life of prayer.

Using the ABC lessons in edification as an index to spiritual growth, let me show by diagram how SLS should be related to these growth levels. I do not intend to promote the notion that your partner's growth will appear systematically before your eyes. However, you will be much more perceptive and helpful if, from time to time, you try to locate where he or she is and give assistance where most needed.

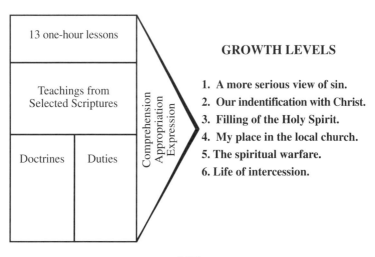

106

Hopefully as you follow the SLS scheme, you will go all around your partner's life bringing encouragement, warning, strengthening wherever needed. It is so tragic that many of our friends are left sinking in their defeats all alone.

Never take for granted the spiritual condition of any person. Keep it fixed in mind that you are to take them through three levels of experience with reference to each truth: (1) Comprehension, (2) Appropriation, (3) Expression.

First of all, you want your partner to have an accurate understanding of the teaching at hand. Does he truly comprehend it? Secondly, has he appropriated, claimed, assimilated this truth into his life and practice? Finally, can he restate it in a simple, winsome way to others so as to affect their living?

Being able to label a teaching is of utmost importance. Some teachings have a primary, direct reference to practice. Other Scripture will deal with doctrine. As you look at a verse, do not merely devotionalize over it. Make a practice of first naming the teaching with an appropriate word or phrase. (Learn the names of various doctrines from any good theology handbook.) Next, you will consider what response you want in your partner's life as you discuss each particular teaching with him. Even those truths which are quite doctrinal in their content should be applied practically to the life. Also, some texts on events have doctrinal implications. To help you evaluate your effectiveness, a checklist of doctrines and duties is provided at the end of this chapter.

Now let us get an overview of all that we are doing. We are using selected Scripture texts to effect new growth in the life of another Christian. This is done through thirteen one-hour sessions of individual ministry. You will be working with various truths in an attempt to get your friend to understand, claim, and share effectively what he receives.

The truths involved are taken directly from the pre-selected texts and they will be looked at from both a doctrinal and a practical point of view. As your partner learns to respond immediately and obediently to each shared truth, he will begin new growth and experience many new blessings in his life. In turn you, the leader, will be much benefited as well.

Coming up in the next chapter will be a thorough examination of the mechanics involved in conducting an SLS.

SLS Leader's Checklist

The following is a survey of some of the key doctrines and life responses covered in the SLS. Used at the conclusion of each session, it will provide a way to evaluate your thoroughness in the studies. By the time the thirteen sessions are concluded, you will have a number of check marks indicating your discussion of most of these matters on several occasions.

Doctrines

___ The person of Christ
___ The death of Christ
___ The Trinity
___ The doctrine of sin
___ The new birth
___ The humanity of Christ
___ Victorious living
___ Scripture
___ Satisfaction in Christ's provisions
___ Return of Christ and the life to come
___ Person and ministries of the Holy Spirit
___ Deity of Christ
___ Activity of Satan
___ Afflictions and trial
___ Prayer in Jesus' name
___ Our identity with Christ
___ Principles of spiritual warfare
___ The resurrection of Christ
___ Release from sin's penalty and relief from its power
___ The transformed life

Practices

___ Witnessing
___ Assurance of Salvation
___ Confession of sin
___ Personal worship
___ Repentance and laying aside of sin habits
___ Daily Bible reading
___ Dedication to service
___ Standing against opposition
___ Ministry to others
___ Being Spirit-filled
___ Godly standards
___ Spiritual warfare
___ Deeper prayer life
___ Self-denial
___ Abiding in Christ
___ Fruit-bearing
___ Family life
___ Baptism
___ Use of spiritual gifts
___ Commitment to the local church

The checklist may be reproduced and used by pastors or others in supervisory capacity as a report sheet of completed SLS. Simply add the following:

SLS Leader _____   Partner _____

Date begun _____   Date completed _____

II
Grasping the Mechanics of This Technique

Now let us go over the actual SLS procedure from start to finish — how to first make arrangements with a prospective partner and then how to conduct a Spiritual Life Study with your friend.

Arranging with a Partner

Most individuals if approached properly will agree readily enough to share in the sessions of fellowship. If you are doubtful about their willingness, then invite them for coffee and have a brief but meaningful devotion time. Suppose you have chosen a well-known Scripture like John 3:16. After reading, you might comment that though the verse is familiar, it holds much spiritual food. Then say, "Let's take a few minutes and share what we discover here. According to the verse, what is God's attitude toward all of us in the world? How much does He love us — according to the verse? What is said here to be the two possible destinies open to all men? What is it that makes the difference? How can one escape damnation?" Then you can point out the nature of faith and what it is to believe *in* Christ. Ask them to note the important word at the center of the verse, then have a time of prayer, giving thanks for the Son of God.

It has been my experience that if a prospective partner is having a wholesome exchange over the Scripture and you have caused God's Word to go through him, so to speak, he will likely desire to repeat such an experience. This is the time to approach him, in this manner:

Immediately after the devotional time, point out how good it is to thus fellowship together, and ask for the privilege of doing so again soon. If he seems agreeable, appoint a time the very next week. Either at next week's meeting or at this

110

first fellowship mention that you have a plan of weekly meetings known as Spiritual Life Studies that have been of great benefit in your life. Offer to share with him. Let him know your keen anticipation of the fellowship. Do not speak of the sessions as a "course" or "John studies" nor present yourself as his "teacher," rather use "partner." Promise to keep the sessions to one hour in length and that they will end after thirteen weeks. Mention that refreshments are not a part of the plan and thus it does not require a protracted portion of any morning or evening — only the one hour. If one of you should have an uncertain schedule, this will present no problem. Since only the two of you are involved, necessary date and time changes can be made as you go along. But try not to skip a week. Of course, the sessions will always be man with man and woman with woman.

Never approach prospects from the point of view that you will merely be giving them what they can pass on to other more needy ones. Rather, make it clear that what you share is for their (and your) benefit.

Your partner will not be given any written material. He must be directed to faithful study of the Scripture in John's Gospel. Perhaps he will want to have daily devotions there. Ask him to give special attention to the first two chapters in preparing for your opening meeting. (No memory verse is assigned until after the first session.)

Preparing to Serve

Yours is a great privilege! Preparation of heart and mind is all important. Expect interruptions, delays, hindrances. God is on your side. You are doing what He orders and He will stand with you.

Then Jesus came to them and said, "All authority in heaven and on earth has been given to me. Therefore go and make disciples of all nations, baptizing them in the name of the Father and of the Son and of the Holy Spirit, and

111

teaching them to obey everything I have commanded you. And surely I am with you always, to the very end of the age" (Matt. 28:18-20).

Some of you will, of course, experience a considerable drag caused by your own natural reticence to be deeply involved with another person. In many cases, the inertia of the standard church program will seem much like a current flowing counter to the kind of spiritual expression SLS brings. Loving patience and persistence is the answer here.

These studies, I am convinced, proceed best when they have little public notice, though the blessing and approval of the church leadership is to be desired. Regardless, strong opposition from Satan should be expected. The leader himself will be glad for many of the teachings shared in various sections dealing with Christian life and warfare.

Before taking up your first regular SLS series, it is imperative that you be thoroughly familiar with all the material in Part 3. The book's introduction and approach section (Part 1) will help you have the proper outlook on the studies and establish a proper relationship with your partner. Then Part 2, which covers the sessions themselves, will become a weekly leader's guide for you. Read it as if you are sitting with me while I work with your friend.

Periodically, you should return to Part 3, checking your own performance and noting carefully any instructions that you may have overlooked or standards that you may have begun to slight.

I will now go over the steps for preparing to lead a session.

Step 1. Read the chapters in John from which the selected teaching texts will come. This will help you know the context of those key verses. There will be no time to teach the context and cover all of the vast riches of this book. However, what you say must be in keeping with the setting of each text. Some will feel strong objections to skipping over many powerful sections of John. But keep in mind our purpose is not to teach this book as such. You are working in a definite field of endeavor where few labor, so give yourself to it and do not wander on inviting bypaths. In fact, you will find it impractical to cover all the Scriptures referred to, not to speak of the many omitted. Rather, you must consider the sessions as a treatment of the total Christian life, using a rapidly moving series of texts during each session. These Scriptures will touch, challenge and throw light on the life from many angles.

Step 2. Read the lesson material given in the Manual, Part 2. Each key Scripture given in the outside margin could be designated in your Bible margin with a tiny circle or "o". You will notice the John verses are discussed in actual order. This will make it easy for you to follow the movement of the lesson without copious notes. If you are both faithful in your preparation and free from the compulsion to say everything that might be said on each point, you should from the outset be able to operate without notes. Even if something is forgotten, you can touch on it next time or in all probability it will come up again in another lesson.

A more accurate way of viewing the studies is to look at your open Bible with the series of tiny marks and realize you will be sharing teachings from God's Word at those particular sites. With your mind and heart filled with the teachings you have reviewed in preparation, the Spirit of God will call to mind what you need as you question your associate regarding his grasp on the truth and what his life response has been.

Notice the questions and instructions in bold type. I have used these again and again in sharing these studies; they have proven effective and bring to light the most

113

essential issues covered in SLS. Your study plan should include circled texts and as many as possible of these highlighted questions.

Step 3. Check the "Additional Teachings" chapter in Part 3. See if there are further teachings you might need to prepare for the upcoming meeting.

Step 4. Review the Manual's final chapter, "Special Helps." Do not copy all this material into your notes for the study session. It is there merely as a refresher to you and to remind you repeatedly of the virtue and possibility of saying sublime things simply.

Step 5. Look at your own notebook to see if there are other things that have blessed and helped you. (Remember, you will add to the notebook new insights as you reread the Manual from the viewpoint of one observing as I minister to a partner.) From time to time, you might also record any truth which is of special benefit in your life — whether from a sermon or your own personal studies or spiritual meditation. As you become more confident and practical in your work, begin developing a list of teachings you feel need to be covered. "Additional Teachings," Chapter III of Part 3, will be suggestive here. You need not be absolutely restricted to this Manual, but make sure things you fit into the schedule of lessons really are essential.

If you feel too helpless without any notes, then limit them to key phrases to jog the memory rather than carrying details that you must repeat. Maintaining a kind of "prepared spontaneity" is important to SLS success.

Conducting the Study

Go with your mind made up to keep within the one-hour time limit. Consider all the areas you wish to touch. Then keep the entire session alive and well trimmed. True, you will pause for special treatment of a truth whenever the Spirit indicates there is need. Remember, avoid the compulsion to "get everything in" and say everything possible on each subject. If you miss something, note it down for your next meeting. You will not need all suggested Scriptures.

Vary your approach slightly with each partner, tailoring the emphasis and applications to each particular person. For example, if you are working with a younger person — maybe your own son or daughter — make many adjustments and keep to a fraction of an hour only. Then after a year or two repeat the studies, upgrading them.

Keep ever in mind that all individuals have needs. If you are meeting with one who is older than you, superior in intelligence and social standing, or beyond you in Christian experience and gifts, do not let that put out your light! If God wants you to share with him, then approach him as you do others with the intention of helping them with their own needs. Under no circumstances should you meet with one simply to share technique and content of teachings that he can pass along to others. Unless SLS brings a "spiritual happening" in the life of your partner, he will not know what to strive for in the lives of those to whom he ministers. Each one should receive the studies deeply into his own heart for his own needs.

Go with a right view of the sessions. As I have suggested before, never refer to them as "Gospel of John studies." Rather, you will be conducting a series of fellowship times with your partner around the Word of God. Your friend should be discouraged from taking many notes. (Many a good truth has been short-circuited through the point of a pen, bypassing the heart.) Avoid calling attention to the Manual or any of the mechanics of this approach. The setting is simply the two of you and the Word of God, meeting in the Name of the Lord.

Constantly ask questions. Ask questions when you suspect they do not know the answer. This prepares them to hear and receive new information. Ask questions when you already know they have the answers. This keeps them alert and participating. (Especially endeavor to incorporate in your conversation the questions in bold type.)

Quite unexpectedly you will come upon blind spots in their thinking and understanding. Even the best of your brothers and sisters will surprise you on occasions with gaping deficiencies. That is precisely why we need one another and why such a wide ranging association as SLS provides is so profitable. So ask questions. In no other way can you discover as much of one's real attitudes, failures, strengths.

Make it a general rule never to leave any given point until your partner has not only understood but appropriated or accomplished it. Often I punctuate a session by actually kneeling in prayer with a friend to help in appropriating one of God's provisions that appears lacking in his life. Keep your times together dynamic and spiritual so that you bring enlightenment and make each lesson genuine in the life.

When it comes to delving into your friend's deeply personal matters, you must keep your balance. Avoid extremes. Just as you will be afraid of being too personal, you must also be afraid of being too indirect and impersonal. On the one hand you will need to keep curiosity in check and not encourage over-ventilation of sin problems. On the other hand you must not fail to give tangible direction and strength to perplexed, defeated brothers in Christ. Never be guilty of a breach of confidence. However, if they are hiding things and appear unwilling to make due restitution, lead them to do so.

Cultivate their confidence to ask you questions, but do not feel under pressure to have all the answers. If God helps

116

you answer, fine. But when you feel uncertain, thank them for the question and mention that you will take it up next time. If a subject arises outside the scope of SLS, ask that it be held until the end of the hour.

Suppose, however, it is something important to them and perhaps on the teaching schedule farther down the line; then what is to be done? There are two extremes: (1) Leave them in the swamp of need until the scheduled moment arrives for help. (2) Allow the sessions to wander in an undisciplined manner at the will of your partner. This breakdown in control can also take place through mixing socializing with your discipline of edification. A pruned vine produces more fruit. Make a judgment each time and stay in charge.

Open each session (after the first) by hearing the assigned memory verse. Do not back down here. Make your partner feel it is expected, normal. It will prove well worth the effort. I have seen people, so lacking in education that they could barely read, learn to memorize precious Scriptures.

At first it will seem awkward having a single individual reciting to you in private. Here is a suggestion for relieving tension: At the very outset, just as you are being seated and before any awkwardness is felt, ask for the memory verse, offering to help whenever memory fails. As time goes on, however, you should tighten down and expect your partner to recite all verses without any prompting, and all should be letter perfect with the Scripture references repeated before and after the verse recitation.

As you finish each session, give them the assignment for next time as indicated in the Manual. If you have assisted them with a particular problem, then you might wish to include an assignment of Scripture search or questions related to the problem area. Sometimes it is especially helpful to add a question or two regarding the next week's lesson.

The Place of Prayer in Each Session

Opening Prayer. Perhaps following the memory verse. Bring your own heart, and your partner's, to the cross. If you feel any agitation, lay it aside in the name of Christ. Earnestly ask for the Spirit's illumination. Also pray again whenever bogged down in a session or a special crisis approaches.

Closing Prayer. Have your friend share in this time to seal the lessons in the heart and ask God's help in practicing each truth.

Personal Intercession. Daily prayer should be made for your partner during this critical three-month experience.

The Final Session — What Next?

Coming to the conclusion of an SLS may be an old and familiar experience to you, but it is quite new to each one going through for the first time. To them, approaching the final session means the ending of something deeply valued. It might also appear as the end of your friendship. It is important they not get the feeling that suddenly you are dropping them. Some will require an easier "let down" by scheduling at least one other meeting in two or three weeks to see how they are doing. Promise to continue in prayer for them. Use the phone once in awhile.

The key word again is balance. You must on the one hand show that you sincerely care and are their friend in Christ, but on the other hand not be so involved that each of you cannot move on into separate, expanding ministries. You should get to others as a leader, and your partner might take up his first study, if you guide him. That is the ideal climax for SLS.

During the course of the last two sessions with your partner, bring up the matter of his sharing this with others.

Promise him that you will stand with him until he becomes an adequate leader. If you judge him able to do this and he is willing, then agree on a friend and proceed. However, he will need regular help from you.

If your partner feels unable to work so systematically with another person, as SLS would demand, commend him nevertheless to a life of edifying others. Quite spontaneously new words and actions of encouragement and helpfulness should issue from his life.

Suggest that he review the entire system of studies, owning his own copy of the Manual and continually stocking a notebook with blessings and insights to share with family and friends.

Before many sessions have been completed, there should be a relationship of sufficient depth that your partner will incline toward your pattern of life. He will want to attend the main meetings of the church as you do — bringing his entire family. Encourage this.

Other Questions in Your Mind

Question: How many different studies should I conduct concurrently?

Answer: As you first begin, take only one. Add a second when you feel confident that you can handle it. Then add others only if you are certain God leads you deeply into this ministry. The work is very demanding, so that most SLS teachers will want to limit themselves to two or three at most. At times, I have carried as many as ten or twelve different studies while responsible for a full schedule of other duties. But such a load would represent an exceptional calling.

Question: What do I do when my partner is quite uncooperative or extremely careless — perhaps missing appointments and declining to do assignments?

119

Answer: Unless your efforts to admonish and stir him change things, it is usually better to terminate the studies. Take the initiative and cut the branch while there is yet some life. Do not let things fizzle out. Say something like, "I am sorry you do not find it possible to continue with the studies right now. If later you have the time and interest, I certainly am willing. Be sure to let me know. I have appreciated getting to know you a little better and will be praying for you." Look at these words again and you will see that they carry a slight reproof in them and the burden of responsibility is placed on the other person where it belongs. This allows conviction to set in and keeps the door open for a more seasonable meeting in the future. I have found very few who want the studies to terminate and some of those who do, ultimately return asking for another opportunity.

III
Additional Teachings

In our course of study together we have discussed many Bible doctrines as they relate to various areas of life. Much has, of course, been left unsaid. The sessions must not be over-filled, and what is taught should elevate the life of the learner.

Purposely, I have not weighted the lessons with large numbers of supporting Bible verses, fearing this might burden leaders to use too many texts. There exists, then, the possibility of your enriching the studies from time to time with Scriptures that have been of recent blessing to you. However, please do not be drawn away into independent bypaths. Complete the sessions on schedule. Invariably, that is the best way.

This chapter contains samplings of further material you might need in working with others. These additional teachings are in two forms: (1) Other areas of Christian living you will want to check on and, (2) Other insights into various Scriptures in the order in which they occur.

These additional teachings are not necessary to be forced into the lessons as you teach them. Rather, they are background helps for deepening your perspective on SLS. For this reason, I have not made regular reference in the main lessons to this section.

Additional Areas of Christian Living to Check

Baptism.   This ordinance was commanded by Jesus and practiced by the Apostles. It must be obeyed. In baptism the believer testifies to his union with Christ and that he has already trusted God for that inner baptism of the Spirit. Study Mark 1:9-11; Acts 2:37-42, 8:36-39; Romans 6:3,4.

The Local Church. Believers meeting in this spiritual fellowship are the very body of Christ on a local scale. Both attendance and responsibilities of service within the fellowship are mandatory (Hebrews 10:24, 25). The believer exercises stewardship of his spiritual gifts and the resources within the local assembly. All the epistles suggest this pattern for the Christian life.

Family worship. Although this must not replace individual devotions, it is of utmost importance that families recognize and honor God together daily. Make practical suggestion for establishing a regular time — perhaps immediately following evening meal, before the family scatters. Encourage them to make the sessions lively, brief, and with some variety. The whole family should be involved in various ways of reading the Scripture, sharing in discussion, praying and singing together. Help them get started.

Husband-Wife Relationships. If the one you are leading in SLS is married, take special notice of his attitude toward the relationship. Apply Scriptural teachings, wherever fitting, to his marriage. Notice the correlation between success in prayer and how people get along with those closest to them, as taught in 1 Peter 3:7-12. In some cases you will want to point out the attitudes and positions to take in order to break any long-standing argument cycle troubling a marriage. See especially 1 Peter 3:8,9.

Additional Insights into the Scripture Lessons

John 4:23, 24. Checking again my definition on worship given under this text, you might find it profitable to underscore the two reasons for worship included in it. These two motives — what God is and what He does — may be seen in other texts such as Psalms 119:68 and 54:6,7. The concept of worship might be made clearer by using one of these texts to see whether your partner can spot two motives for worship, and then relate them to the main definition. The use of a Scripture such as Psalm 31:14, reading the verse and affirming it aloud in prayer, will do the heart much good.

John 5. Following up on last week's worship emphasis, open this third SLS lesson using Psalm 103 in a time of unitied worship.

John 5:14. As I intimated in the previous chapter, it is important as you approach the matter of one's personal sin to keep your own heart clear of any evil curiosity on the one hand and on the other not to be neutralized by oversensitivity. There are many desperately needy people who will respond to a steady word of guidance. It was not particularly pleasant for Jesus to take hold of His disciples' feet and wash them. Some tasks simply cannot be done with a ten-foot pole!

A good approach is to ask: Is there a continuing failure in sin from which you cannot seem to gain release? Then before they answer, if you like, tactfully add, "I do not need to know exactly what it is, but let me know if there is, then I can at least stand with you in prayer."

I strongly suggest that you read carefully Chapter 4 entitled "Special Help: The Deliverance Encounter" in my book *People Helping People: How Every Christian Can Counsel*, published by the author. Permit me to share the riddle with which the chapter opens:

Suppose a man has committed the same sin 499 times. He has confessed the sin 498 times. Now, what is the one thing this man really needs? (Stop and think it over a few moments before reading on.)

You may further suppose the man has made his confession as honestly as he knows how, even to the

123

point of tears, and that he really wants to be free. Now what is it he needs? True enough, God requires that he make confession number 499. But God also offers something more than what he is experiencing. If not, then sin number 500 is surely coming up!

Quite obviously if you meet up with such a case, you will want your encounter to have an element of "showdown." Prepare faithfully by studying the pertinent material offered in the Manual, and may God assist you in bringing liberation. That is what is needed.

John 6:9. As they respond to your question and instructions, if you sense any self-pity, remember there is sometimes a subtle rebellion even in hopelessness. See Jeremiah 18:12. Be careful and loving but also be perceptive and discerning.

In light of Philippians 4:13, where do they stand on the "confidence scale?" At one extreme some feel "I can't do anything." At the other extreme some feel "I can do all things" — even without Christ's help. It is not enough to avoid the pride involved in the second extreme statement. We must also avoid the first extreme. The man who makes his particular case of inadequacy so difficult and special is also exposing his selfish concern. The rebellion of passiveness might turn up in one with whom you deal, whether teacher or church leader.

John 6:47-58. Jesus is not here commanding participation in Communion or the Lord's Supper. It might at first sound so but that is only because the Upper Room celebration and the John 6 passage are both teaching the same lesson; namely, that believers must by faith share in Christ's life and death for them. John 6 is not pointing at the Upper Room but at Calvary. It might be diagramed as indicated on the next page.

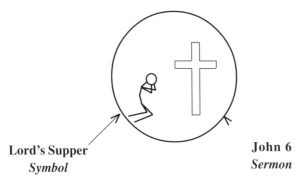

Lord's Supper   **John 6**
Symbol   *Sermon*

John 7:37-29. By no means are all God's blessings transmitted to us in private, directly from His hand to our hearts. Much of the vital flow from Jesus Christ as Head of the church gets to His various members through one another. Sometimes a diagram will be of use as you bring this instruction. Here are two I use on occasion:

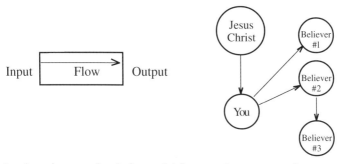

My drawing at the left could be used to strengthen your emphasis. You might ask: If this section of pipe represents your life as a channel of blessing through which God's blessings flow into other lives, at which end must the channel be plugged in order to stop the flow? Obviously, at either end. Where do most believers place their major concern? All too many forget their output into other lives, not realizing their reception of further blessings from God will also cease if they are not faithful in transmitting the vital flow to others in spiritual ministries.

125

A little reflection on the second diagram will probably bring truths to mind. "Now to each one the manifestation of the Spirit is given for the common good" (1 Corinthians 12:7). Thus it is that God equips and blesses you, and you in turn are responsible to edify other believers. Still further, some of them (Believer #2) can reach out where you cannot (Believer #3).

John 9:1-3. I suggest including the discussion indicated in this text even when your partner is not presently in a trial. Afflictions have a way of coming sooner or later. Furthermore, one of your aims is to equip him for helping those in his circle of acquaintance who might be in need of understanding and comfort — perhaps one in his immediate family or in his Sunday School class or where he works.

John 9:25. You will have opportunities to encourage personal evangelism when covering John 1 and John 4. As the subject of witnessing comes up yet again you should press the matter very definitely this time. Mention that a good question to use when inquiring about a friend's trust in Christ is: If God asked you, "What right have to enter heaven?" what would you answer? This is a very incisive inquiry and helps uncover a person's real foundation.

Teach your partner how to use everyday conversation as opportunities for witnessing. For example, upon hearing one complain of some problem, a Christian might interject, "I used to fall apart under such difficulties until I discovered what it was to be a real Christian." Usually, a burdened friend will follow up on such a statement by asking what you mean.

John 10. You might be helped personally in your soul-shepherding by studying Ezekiel 34.

John 10:1-16. Regarding Satan's voice as it troubles the sheep, remember his devices are many. Not only does he

126

use the element of allurement in temptation, but on occasion a kind of repulsion might be used to back a believer away from something or someone good. Other devices are insinuation, accusation, division, distortion or misrepresentation and an endless variety of deceptions. The devil truly is the father of lies.

You will need God's help in determining whether the trouble symptoms you might notice indicate simply carnal weakness or a deeper advantage being taken by the enemy. Notice any excessive moodiness, passive unwillingness to make choices and claim God's help, an enslaved will, distorted self-image, oversensitivity toward others' opinions, uncontrollable appetites, superstitious or occult tendencies of any form, habitually troubled sleep, nagging doubts, overactive imagination or driven thought life, compulsive and erratic behavior.

The faithful pursuit of Spiritual Life Studies generally brings much relief in these problem areas. As an example, take the matter of the partner with troubled sleep. Such a one should be encouraged to commit himself to the Lord each night as he retires, using Scripture promises and prayer. Pray with him specifically and get him started memorizing Scripture that he can quote and meditate on as he lies in bed. A deep healing is in prayer, Scripture and the kind of fellowship that you will offer.

John 10:3-8, 26-27. Read very carefully. All these verses indicate why some of Jesus' hearers did not understand and believe, whereas His own true sheep would respond to their Shepherd's voice. Obedient response is characteristic of a true believer. Herein lies two substantial helps for you as you attempt to counsel others:

(1) Your own encouragement. If in the Shepherd's name you speak His word to His sheep, they will respond as He says.

(2) Here is also the tool of truth which you will use. Read these verses to your friend, placing him, as it were at the fork of decision. Then ask, "Will you now heed what your Shepherd says to you?"

John 14:16. A simple diagram often helpful to me follows:

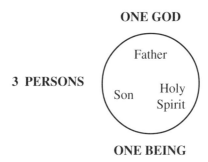

After sketching the picture above, write down the following on another paper:

One   _____

Three   _____

Ask them to fill in the blanks, indicating in what sense God is One and in what sense He may be said to be Three. Of course the answers are One *Being*, Three *Persons.* Point out how important it is to maintain the plurality of the Trinity without denying the unity of God. And also, how important it is to maintain the unity without destroying distinction between the Persons of the Godhead. Stay simple and prayerful and God will in time make it understandable to them.

128

Romans 6, 7, 8. A brief orientation relating to habit-type sins might prove helpful. Three serious ailments result from such practices.

(1) The carnal mind is seriously stimulated and strengthened.

(2) The will is weakened and crippled.

(3) Often a deception develops within the thinking of the person so that he becomes very inaccurate in his understanding of the condition.

Habits might begin when what one *wants* is chosen above what one *knows* to be right. Once a pattern of yielding to wrong desire or evil expression of any kind is established, a slavery sets in. This may be accompanied by a deceiving rationalization until what is wrong seems right, or at least excusable. Ultimately, sinful desire or passions rule the mind, and the will is unable to break free.

Sometimes it all begins when the victim is offered by the tempter some pittance of pleasure — just enough to get him to indulge. Such a choice repeated often enough will thoroughly confuse the volition's equilibrium. Eventually, some victims of habitual sin or outbreaks of passion discover they are not so much attracted to the evil expression as driven to continue. No longer are they "rewarded" but feel so upset and agitated that yielding to the sin becomes an escape from torment. The torment is accentuated by the stark realization, "I can't stop!" Finally, they are driven to indulge in order to forget they are driven. And thus, the enslavement is complete. The dependency which began as a chemical, physical, or emotional one might end up as an evil-spirit bondage, wherein one is virtually forced into participation in order to put out the raging fire of inner anguish.

However, the weapons of our warfare are entirely adequate — both to help ourselves and also for us to use in ministering to others. "For though we live in the world, we do not wage war as the world does. The weapons we fight with are not the weapons of the world. On the contrary, they have divine power to demolish strongholds. We demolish arguments and every pretension that sets itself up against the knowledge of God, and we take captive every thought to make it obedient to Christ" (2 Cor. 10:3-5). What are these spiritual weapons?

First of all the Word of God is the very sword of the Spirit and is "living and active. Sharper than any double-edged sword, it penetrates even to dividing soul and spirit, joints and marrow; it judges the thoughts and attitudes of the heart" (Heb. 4:12).

Next, there is the power of prayer whereby we may exert a spiritual influence on the needy heart or, if necessary, bind and resist Satan in the name of Jesus Christ. In addition, we may claim the Holy Spirit — and greater is He Who is in us than he who is in the world (1 John 4:4).

Added to this should be the basic understanding of truths taught in Romans 6, 7, 8. See my teachings in the final three lessons, also the Manual at John 5:14. For more extensive treatment of gaining release from slavery to sin, see the chapter entitled "Deliverance Encounter" in *People Helping People*.

IV
Special Helps for Saying It Simply

1. Triune God

God is a three-Person Being. Man is a single-person being. (Surely, it is not surprising to learn that God is different from man.) There is ONE God (Deuteronomy 6:4). He is *not* three different beings. However, it is proper to think of the three Persons (Father, Son and Holy Spirit) as distinct. Distinct Persons and yet unified in the one God. Our God is Tri-unity. The Father loved the world and gave the Son. The Son took on a body of flesh and died for us. The Holy Spirit applies the benefits of redemption to us.

Each believer is provided the Spirit's inner baptism (John 1:33; Acts 2:32, 33, 38, 39; 1 Corinthians 12:13). Since this is true, the Spirit's fullness should be claimed pointedly by the church for each convert and claimed by the converts for themselves. Then, daily the Christian must allow the Spirit's filling in his life (Ephesians 5:18).

2. Sin

The entire human race is in a fallen, sinful condition. A child may claim only the inheritance his father provides. Our father Adam was led into sin by Satan's wiles. The cloud of guilt has settled over all men. Universally, men tend to sin, resisting whatever degree of light they may receive in their conscience, through creation or from revelation of Scripture. The very Son of God was once crucified, and He is still being neglected and rejected today (John 1:10, 11; 3:18-20).

Sin is a broad subject. The term "sin" is used in three different ways in the bible.

131

(1) *Sin as legal guilt.** Romans 3:9 and Galatians 3:22 state that we are all counted legally under guilt. The record reads "guilty." The penalty is death. This death sentence is executed first in our character (inner defilement, carnality) and next in our bodies (ailments and aging leading to the grave).

(2) Sin as *inner corruption, defilement* (Romans 7:17). Just as this carnal nature comes as a punishment of guilt (above), so our wrongdoings (below) come out of this inner condition of pollution.

(3) Sin as *wrong actions*: Omissions (James 4:17) and commissions (1 John 3:4). These may be in word, thought or deed.

A central purpose of all these studies is to show how our Savior delivers us from sin. Great victory can be ours.

*Note: As you ask people to write out their definition of sin, they will usually have difficulty with sin as legal guilt. Ask them to think of another word to substitute in the two verses here for the word "sin." Synonyms for sin are condemnation, judgment, damnation or guilt in the legal sense. (Romans 4:8 might get you "in gear.")

3. **End Time Events***

(1) At physical death the believer's soul goes directly to be with the Lord. Cf. Luke 23:43; 2 Corinthians 5:6, 8; Philippians 1:21-23. These departed spirits will return with Jesus later.

(2) Jesus Christ will return to gather His children (Matthew 24:21-31). Deceased saints and those still alive will be given new bodies (1 Corinthians 15:49-52; Philippians 3:20-21). Oh, may we be prepared to welcome Him with joy (1 John 2:28; 3:3)!

(3) Christ will for a time rule the earth, reigning with His saints. This period is popularly called the Millennium.

(4) Finally, the wicked dead will be raised for the great judgment (Revelation 20). This will be followed by the eternal separation of men. See Revelation 20:15 and chapter 21.

*Note: Some Bible passages compress all these events until they appear as a single episode. Indeed, some Old Testament texts appear to picture Christ's first coming in flesh and the final judgment both in one sweep. Other Scriptures, however, enrich the picture with details, perhaps treating only a single phase of the last events.

4. The Transformed Life of the Believer

General

The Christian is different. He is Christ-like in his daily life at home, in the community, school or business. Even his inner thoughts change. Lusts and self-centeredness are put down, and the harsh, irritable disposition toward others is replaced by a gracious, considerate concern. "Love one another," commands Jesus. This includes those who may ridicule and make things difficult because of your Christian life.

Characteristics of This New Life

(1) Obedience — Our life is to be committed to Christ. We are to follow, obey, keep in fellowship with Him. Once knowing something to be His will, we must obey.

(2) Faith — A confident trust in the Lord; not ruled by our own feelings. Our emotional life may rise and fall, but the One in Whom we have come to trust never changes. Faith looks to Jesus, not just at threatening circumstances. Note how Peter fell when he began to look away from the Lord (Matthew 14:22-31). If a brooding discouragement persists, the following questions must be faced:

(a) Have I been disobedient to Christ?

(b) If so, have I made full confession and turned away from the sin? See Psalm 32.

(c) Or, are these feelings merely accusations from Satan to destroy my confidence in Christ?

(4) Joy — This is not mere feeling. It is a tide of well-being based on the truth. Our outlook is bright because we are on the "winning side." Christ is ever with us (Matthew 28:20). The fellowship can be continuous (1 John 1:7). See Peter 1:8.

How to Decide What is Right and Wrong — Questionable Things

(1) First, settle the matter once and for all that you will set your life by teachings of Scripture, not by ways of the world (Romans 12:1, 2; 2 Corinthians 6:14-18). Though you remain in society you will not wrongly conform to it and share in certain of its worldly functions. Things named in the Bible as wrong are to be dropped. The Christian is also obligated to obey the Spirit as He leads us to see any other things as harmful. We may apply certain tests to a matter in question:

(2) Tests

(a) Will this harm me?

My body (1 Corinthians 6:19,20)?

My freedom of will by perhaps binding me in a habit (1 Corinthians 6:12)?

My testimony (Romans 12:17)?

My love-relation with Christ (Ephesians 4:30)?

(b) Will it harm others, misleading them in any way (Romans 14:13-21; 1 Corinthians 8:9-13; Matthew 18:6, 7)?

(c) Would Jesus do this? We must follow Him (1 Peter 2:21).

(3) Finally, Romans 14:22, 23 suggests: If in doubt, don't.

Conclusion

The life that is more set on struggling for its old ways, habits and pleasures than on pleasing the Lord of glory has seen little of its own sin and needs, and little of His glory.

5. Satan

The devil is called in Scripture the prince or god of the present world (John 14:30; 2 Corinthians 4:4). Apparently, he fell from his heavenly place because of rebellion. He employs a kingdom of evil spirits who likewise are in rebellion against God.

Besides his grip on the wicked, Satan's hosts assault the children of God. Though this is done in the greatest of wrath and malice (1 Peter 5:8), it is usually done with subtlety and deception (2 Corinthians 11:3, 14).

This inner working against the children of God might come in the form of some attraction toward sin, or it might take any of countless forms — all calculated to discourage the Christian and make him unfruitful. This is best accomplished by the enemy when the believer allows him a foothold in the life (cf. John 14:30) through ignorance and failure to resist (2 Corinthians 2:11; Ephesians 6:10-18; 1 Peter 5:9; James 4:7).

Notes: